FINISH LINE
Reading
for the Common Core State Standards

Continental

Acknowledgments

Illustrations: Page 8: Doris Ettlinger; Page 25: Harry Norcross; Page 31, 36, 41, 47, 49, 106, 124, 140, 143, 165, 181, 182, 195, 201, 206, 212: Laurie Conley; Page 62: Jane Yamada; Page 74: Dennis Bond; Page 159: Marty Husted; Page 194: Deborah C. Johnson

Photographs: Page 8: © Tkachev Andrei/TAR-TASS/Corbis; Page 16: www.shutterstock.com, Paul B. Moore; Page 29: www.shutterstock.com, Olga Bogatyrenko; Page 34: Edvard Munch; Page 44: Francis M. Fritz; Page 58: Library of Congress, Prints and Photographs Division, Carl Van Vechten Collection, LC-USZ62-120746; Page 67: Library of Congress, Prints and Photographs Division, LC-USZ62-40054; Page 70: Library of Congress, Prints and Photographs Division, LC-USZC4-11941; Page 95: www.istockphoto.com/Elena Korenbaum; Page 98: © Royalty-Free/Corbis; Page 100: Library of Congress, Prints and Photographs Division, LC-USF344-007933-ZB; Page 114: Image used under Creative Commons from Kristof vt; Page 130: Image used under Creative Commons from Dave Bunnell; Page 131: Image used under Creative Commons from Daniel Jackson; Page 135 border: www.shutterstock.com, Natalie Barsukova; Page 135 *SUE:* Image used under Creative Commons from Fritz Geller-Grimm; Page 135 *cake:* C Squared Studios; Page 136: Image used under Creative Commons from J. Nguyen; Page 150: Library of Congress, Prints and Photographs Division, LC-USZ61-791; Page 167: www.photos.com; Page 170 *photograph 1:* National Park Service; Page 170 *photograph 2:* Library of Congress, Prints and Photographs Division, LC-USZ62-121165; Page 170 *photograph 3:* www.istockphoto.com/Michael Thompson; Page 177: Tracy Montana/PhotoLink; Page 185: NASA/Hasselblad; Page 186: NASA; Page 190: Library of Congress, Prints and Photographs Division, U.S. News & World Report Magazine Collection, LC-DIG-ppmsca-03130; Page 208: Image used under Creative Commons from Paulo Juntas; Page 215: U.S. Navy photo by Chief Intelligence Specialist Louis Fellerman/Released; Page 216: Library of Congress, Prints and Photographs Division, LC-DIG-ppprs-00626

Table of Contents

Welcome to Finish Line Reading for the Common Core State Standards

This book will give you practice in the reading and comprehension skills necessary to be an effective reader. It will also help you to prepare for reading tests that assess your skills and knowledge.

The material in this book is aligned to the Common Core State Standards for English Language Arts and Literacy in History, Social Studies, Science, and Technical Subjects. The Common Core State Standards (CCSS) build on the education standards developed by the states. The CCSS "specify what literacy skills and understandings are required for college and career readiness in multiple disciplines." This book will help you practice the skills necessary to be a literate person in the 21st century.

In the lessons of this book, you will read informational and literary selections and then answer multiple-choice and short-response questions about them. The lessons in this book are in three parts:

- The first part introduces the reading skill you are going to study and explains what it is and how you use it.

- The second part is called Guided Practice. You will get more than just practice here; you will get help. You will read a story, poem, or nonfiction article and answer questions about it. After each question, you will find an explanation of the correct answer. So you will answer questions and find out right away if you were correct. You will also learn why one answer is correct and others are not.

- The third part is called Test Yourself. Here you will read a passage and answer the questions on your own.

When you finish each unit, you will complete a Review Lesson to show what you have learned in that unit. This will help you evaluate the progress you are making. After you have finished all of the lessons and units, you will take a Practice Test at the end of the book.

Now you are ready to begin using this book. Good Luck!

Vocabulary Development

You use words all the time. This unit is all about vocabulary development. You will learn the meanings of new words and how to use them.

- **In Lesson 1,** you will learn to figure out the meanings of new words when you read them. Sometimes words will have more than one meaning. You will learn how to tell which meaning is correct. Then you will learn how to add extra parts to words to make new words.

- **Lesson 2** is about knowing the difference between different ways of saying things. Sometimes words mean exactly what they say. Sometimes they take on different meanings. You will learn to tell the difference.

- **Lesson 3** is about those words that you may only read about in science or social studies. You will learn how to use clues to discover the meanings of special terms.

Now turn the page and start building your vocabulary!

Word Meanings

L.3.4, RL.3.4, RI.3.4

Think back to when you were very young. You pointed and asked, "What's that?" And you listened when people answered you. You learned words from TV and songs. You figured out what words meant by how they related and connected to the words you already knew. This is called using **context clues.**

You are older now and can read. Now you figure out the meaning of new words using context clues in sentences or paragraphs.

Context Clues

Read the following sentence from J.M. Barrie's *Peter Pan.*

Cecco was the bravest of all Hook's men, but this time he hesitated.

Do you know what the word <u>hesitated</u> means? If not, you can figure it out. Just look at the words and ideas in the sentence. You have one good context clue. It says that Cecco was the bravest. Then the author uses the word, *but.* This means that this time Cecco is not so brave. <u>Hesitate</u> means "to pause." You can guess that the word <u>hesitated</u> means that he stopped being brave and paused.

Context clues may come in several forms:

Context Clues

Synonyms	Words that have about the same meanings
Examples	Words that show what another word means
Definitions	Words that tell what another word means
Descriptions	Words that tell you more about a word, by comparing or explaining

Synonyms

Words in a sentence may mean about the same thing. You may know one word. Then you can figure out the other.

Using knives and forks became popular in the Middle Ages. Those who used them were well-liked and admired.

The words well-liked and admired both explain that using knives and forks was a good thing. Say you didn't know the meaning of well-liked. You could figure out from the context that it means basically the same as admired.

Examples

Sometimes you learn what words mean through example. There may be an unknown word. Then there will be an example of the unknown word to help you understand.

Dr. Leung, the cardiologist, ran tests and X-rays on her aunt's heart.

What does cardiologist mean? The context shows that it's a noun. The -ologist ending suggests that a cardiologist is a scientist or doctor. The example explains how the doctor ran tests on a heart. You can figure out that cardiologist means "a doctor or scientist who works with hearts."

Definitions

An unknown word is sometimes defined in context. Look for definition in these sentences:

Showing compassion to a ladybug, Matt moved the bug away from the spider's web.

You may have heard the word compassion. However, you may not have had to read it. You can tell that the word is an adjective. It describes Matt's action. However, the sentence gives you the definition. The context tells you that compassion means "helping others in need."

Descriptions

Sometimes a sentence will describe what a word means. It might *compare* something you know. Or, it might connect between a new word and ones you know.

> Susie missed the goal five times, but the team supported her trying by clapping and cheering.

You may not know the word <u>supported</u>. But you can compare the way the team acted in the sentence. The team was clapping and cheering. This means that they all like Susie for trying. <u>Supported</u> means "helping."

> Ken rotated his hula hoop in large circles around his hips.

The word <u>rotated</u> may be new to you. However, you probably have heard of a hula hoop. You know how to make large circles. So you can figure out what <u>rotated</u> means. You can *connect* what you know. A hula hoop moves around your body. <u>Rotated</u> must mean something about moving around in circles.

Guided Practice

Read the passage. Then answer the questions.

In Siberia, a man was walking with his deer. He came across something strange. It was the remains of an animal. It was a baby <u>mammoth</u>—an elephantlike animal that lived long ago! This <u>fossil</u> is the most complete we have yet. We cannot see the animal when it was living. However, the fossil helps us see what it once was. The fossil shows us the remains of the animal.

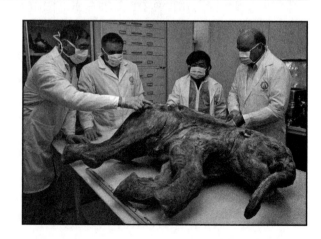

The baby mammoth body was frozen in a layer of permafrost. This kind of frigid coldness helped to create the fossil. Permafrost is the layer of frozen soil that is always frozen. It is hard for anything to decay or waste away. That is one reason the mammoth's body was kept in one piece for so long.

Scientists named the mammoth Lyuba. As they study Lyuba, they hope the remains will help us. We still want to know what happened to all the mammoths 10,000 years ago.

Make sure you know the exact meaning of the new words in this passage. You can check their meaning in a print or online dictionary.

A mammoth is a ____.

   A large animal still living to this day

   B dinosaur creature that was killed by hunters

   C large animal that lived thousands of years ago

   D small animal that ate lots of plants and weeds

Understanding the word mammoth involves making a *comparison* in your mind. The passage says that mammoths were "elephantlike." Elephants are large. The passage also says that mammoths lived long ago. Choice A says that they were large animals. But choice A also says that they are still living to this day. That is not correct. The correct answer is choice C.

A fossil is ____.

   A a mammoth

   B something old

   C a frozen animal

   D an animal's remains

You need to find a *synonym* for fossil. In paragraph 1, you find that a fossil is the "remains." This is a synonym. The word *remains* means almost the same as fossil. Choice D is the correct answer.

The word <u>frigid</u> means ____.

   A icy coldness

   B weather changes

   C burning heat

   D breezy chill

If you do not know what <u>frigid</u> means you can figure it out. Look at how the word is *described.* Paragraph 2 talks about coldness and ice. This is your clue. It does not talk about heat, breezes, or weather changes. The correct answer is choice A.

<u>Permafrost</u> is a science term in the passage. Use all the information in the passage. Then tell in your own words what this word means.

_____

_____

_____

You need to look at paragraph 2 closely. <u>Permafrost</u> is defined well. You just need to retell the meaning in your own words. Here is a sample answer:

<u>Permafrost</u> is a layer of soil that is frozen. It is so icy that animal bodies can freeze in the <u>permafrost</u>. Their bodies still remain, but they are in a frozen state.

Words With Multiple Meanings

Some words have two or more meanings. This can get tricky. A dictionary will list each meaning. The dictionary will place numbers in front of the different meanings. Most of the time, the different meanings are spelled alike. You even say them the same way. However, if you don't know all the meanings, you will not understand what you are reading. Here are some of the many meanings of the word <u>fair</u>:

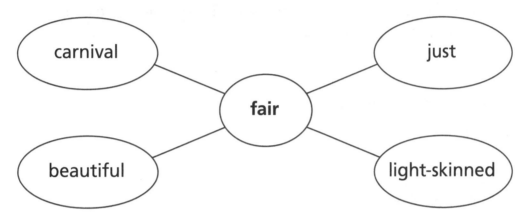

Say you come across a word like <u>fair</u> in a sentence. You have to use context clues. Only then can you find out its meaning. First, see how it is used in the sentence. What part of speech is it? Is it a verb (action word)? Is it a noun (the name of a person, place, or thing)? Or is it an adjective (a word that describes)?

The judge was <u>fair</u> in picking out the winner of the contest.

You can tell in this sentence that <u>fair</u> is an adjective. Which of the meanings shown above are adjectives? There are three of them. But which fits the sentence best? The one that makes the most sense is "just."

Guided Practice

Do you like the feeling of bouncing a rubber <u>ball</u>? Many people think that Mayans were the first to make rubber balls. They think they made these as early as 1600 B.C. Mayans made the rubber with sap from the rubber tree. The first rubber balls were the size of a beach ball. They were over 15 <u>pounds</u>. The Mayans played a game with them. The game was a <u>cross</u> between football and basketball.

The word <u>ball</u> in this passage means _____.

   A a special dance

   B a round bouncing sphere

   C a good time, or blast

   D a royal party with dancing

As used in the passage, the word <u>ball</u> is a noun. All of the answers are nouns. That clue will not help you. Instead, read each answer carefully. Do any of the answers have to do with rubber or games? The best answer is "round bouncing sphere." It does not mean a dance or good time in this passage. Choice B is the correct answer.

What is meant by <u>pounds</u> in this passage?

A to batter something

B to hit with the hand

C a weight

D to smash into something

<u>Pounds</u> may have any of these meanings. See how it is used. Did the passage say anything about the Mayans hitting the balls? No. It just said how the balls were made. Look at the sentence before the one with <u>pounds</u>. It talks about the size of the ball. We know that the passage is talking about weight. Choice C is the correct answer.

What are some different meanings of the word <u>cross</u>? Which meaning is the best meaning of <u>cross</u> for this passage?

_____

_____

_____

_____

_____

Read the last sentence again. Here is a sample answer:

<u>Cross</u> could mean angry. To <u>cross</u> something means to go over it. Someone could make a <u>cross</u> by putting two sticks together. Here the word <u>cross</u> means a mixture of two things. The two things that are crossed are football and basketball.

Using Prefixes, Suffixes, and Root Words

Words often have smaller parts. You can learn new words because you already know many smaller parts. A **prefix** is a part of a word added to the beginning of the word. It changes the meaning of the word. You know the word lucky, and you know that the prefix *un-* means "not." Now you can figure out that unlucky means "not lucky."

A **suffix** is a part added to the end of a word that changes the meaning of the word. You know the word care, and you know that the suffix *-less* means "without." You can figure out that careful means "without care."

Most prefixes and suffixes come from Latin and Greek words. For example, the prefix *tri-* comes from the Latin word for "three." Think of the word *tricycle.* It has three wheels!

Some Common Prefixes

Prefix	Meaning	Example
bi-	two	bicycle
de-	opposite	defrost
dis-	not	disagree
in-/im-	in or not	inexpensive
mid-	middle	midnight
non-	no, not, without	nonfiction
pre-	before	preview
re-	back, again	replay
un-	not	unpleasant

Some Common Suffixes

Suffix	Meaning	Example
-able	able to	agree<u>able</u>
-ance	state or action	entr<u>ance</u>
-er	one who does something	danc<u>er</u>
-ful	full of, likely to	rest<u>ful</u>
-less	without	humor<u>less</u>
-ly	like, in the manner of	usual<u>ly</u>
-ness	the state of	happi<u>ness</u>
-ology	study of	myth<u>ology</u>
-y	like or tending to	stick<u>y</u>

You can make new words! Prefixes and suffixes may be added to **root words.** If you know the meaning of a root word, it helps. And if you know the meaning of a prefix or suffix, it helps to figure out a word.

Many English words have Greek and Latin roots. For instance, the Latin root <u>cycle</u> means "wheel or circle." From the prefix list, you know that *bi-* means "two." The word <u>bicycle</u> means "two wheels."

Some Common Greek and Latin Roots

Root Word	Meaning	New Word	New Word Meaning
auto	self	automobile	self-moving
aqua	water	aquarium	water-filled enclosure
bio	life	biology	study of life
cycle	wheel, circle	unicycle	a bike with one wheel
geo	earth	geography	writing about the earth
graph	write, draw	autograph	self-writing
leg	law	legal	relating to the law
port	carry, bring	airport	place where people are brought by airplane

Guided Practice

Read the passage. Then answer the questions.

Vikings

What made Vikings so <u>powerful</u>? Many people wonder this. But if you look closely, you will see. Vikings were great sailors. And they were the best shipbuilders at the time. They used sails and oars in their boats. So the ships went very fast. The ships could also sail up and down rivers quickly. The boats were also light enough to be <u>transported</u> across land. Nobody quite knew when a Viking attack might come. Even the strongest armies could not <u>prepare</u>. These towns were taken over.

The suffix -*ful* in <u>powerful</u> means _____.

    A tiny

    B some

    C a little

    D a lot of

> After you read, you know that Vikings had a lot of power.
> You know that -*ful* means "full of." Something that is "full of"
> probably has "a lot of." Choice D is the correct answer.

The prefix *pre-* in <u>prepare</u> means _____.

    A over

    B above

    C after

    D before

> You could look at the chart and know *pre-* means "before." Or,
> you could look at the word in context. If the armies could not
> prepare ahead of time, they were taken over. Choice D is the
> correct answer.

Look at the prefix and root in <u>transport</u>. What does the word mean?

_____

> You know what the root <u>port</u> means. Just check the root chart.
> You can find the prefix *trans-* on the prefix chart. Here is a sample
> answer:

    <u>Transport</u> means "to carry something across."

Test Yourself

In 1844, Elizabeth Blackwell went to see a sick friend. This woman had a terrible <u>illness</u>. Her friend said to her, "Why do you not <u>study medicine</u>?" The woman said she wished for a female doctor.

Elizabeth told her that women were not allowed to be doctors. It was not <u>proper</u> at the time. Women could not know anything about how the human body works.

After awhile, Elizabeth thought about her friend. She thought how unfair it was. She was just as smart as any man. Women needed female doctors.

Elizabeth tried to get into 29 schools. She even thought about <u>disguising</u> herself as a man. But she knew she needed to open the doors for other women.

At last, one school in New York let her enter. She finished at the <u>head</u> of her class. She went on to open a <u>clinic</u> for the poor. Here, Elizabeth <u>treated</u> people. She was a teacher, too. She taught classes on the <u>importance</u> of exercise. She also taught people about <u>hygiene</u>. People needed to learn how to keep their body clean and free from germs.

Elizabeth's small clinic became larger. It became more like a hospital. It was also a college. Today, there are many female doctors. But the very first <u>pioneer for women</u> was Elizabeth Blackwell.

1 The suffix *-ness* in <u>illness</u> means _____.

   A doing

   B acting

   C state of

   D wanting

Check your answers by looking up the meanings of the underlined words in a print or online dictionary.

2 What does the friend mean when she says Elizabeth should <u>study medicine</u>?

_____

_____

_____

_____

3 <u>Proper</u> means _____.

   A know it all

   B wants it all

   C wrong and rude

   D polite and correct

4 Think about the word <u>disguise</u>. Why does Elizabeth think about <u>disguising</u> herself as a man?

_____

_____

_____

_____

5 The word <u>head</u> has many different meanings. In paragraph 5, what is the correct meaning of <u>head</u>?

   A top

   B skull

   C lead

   D travel

6 The word <u>clinic</u> means _____.

   A class

   B workshop

   C health center

   D meeting place

7 The word <u>treat</u> has many different meanings. In paragraph 5, which phrase could *best* replace <u>treated</u>?

   A paid for

   B cared for

   C delighted

   D dealt with

8 The word <u>importance</u> has a prefix, root, and suffix. Look back to the charts on pages 14–16. Give the definition for each word part.

_____

_____

_____

_____

_____

9 What does the word <u>hygiene</u> mean in paragraph 5?

   A taking a bath

   B staying dirty

   C keeping clean of germs

   D knowing how to use medicine

10 American pioneers traveled west. They faced hardships. However, they led the way for others to travel west. What does the phrase <u>pioneer for women</u> mean in the last paragraph?

_____

_____

_____

_____

_____

Word Relationships

L.3.5, RL.3.4, RI.3.4

You know that words can have more than one meaning. Did you know that words could have *shades* of meaning? *Shades* is one of those words with more than one meaning. It can mean something you put over windows. It can mean lightness or darkness of color. It can even mean sunglasses. What does the word *shades* have to do with words?

Figurative Language

Literal language is used to give information. We use **figurative language** to play with language. Writers use figurative language to describe things. It helps you see, feel, hear, or understand things. "There was a full moon" is a literal statement. It simply tells you that the moon was full and round. Now read this next sentence. "The gray moon was like a cold nickel shining in the dark clouds." This lets you *see* and *feel* the moon.

Read this next line of "The Months of the Year" by Sara Coleridge:

> March brings breezes loud and shrill,
> Stirs the dancing daffodil.

You have to ask a few questions here. Can a month bring breezes? Can daffodils dance? No. We know this is figurative language. There are special words we use for figurative language. See the chart on the next page.

Personification	a writer gives human qualities to things	dancing daffodils
Simile	a writer uses the words *like* or *as* to compare two things	the moon *was like* a cold nickel
Metaphor	a writer compares two unlike things *without* using *like* or *as*	the moon *was* a cold nickel

Figurative language is important. Writers can paint pictures with words. Or, they can just state things plainly. You need to know when an author is using figurative or literal language. If you can't figure it out, you may be confused.

Elements of Poetry

There is rich figurative language in **poetry.** Many poets like to paint word pictures. Often this is done through the senses—touch, taste, smell, hear, and see.

Every poem has a **speaker.** The speaker in the poem gives ideas and a point of view. Sometimes the speaker is the poet, and sometimes it is a made-up character.

Many poems have **rhyme**—repeated sounds at the ends of words. Sometimes the rhyme comes at the ends of a line of poetry, as, for example, in this old **limerick:**

*There was an old man from **Peru**
Who dreamed he was eating his **shoe.**
He woke in a **fright**
In the middle of the **night**
And found it was perfectly **true.***

Sometimes rhyming words appear in the same line:

> **Tom, Tom,** the piper's **son**
> Stole a pig and away did **run**
> The pig was **eat,** and Tom was **beat,**
> And Tom ran crying down the **street.**

Many poems have no rhyme at all, like this **haiku** poem:

> Jumping frog, happy frog,
> Sitting on a lily pad,
> Eating a new catch.

Rhythm is the pattern of beats. In poems, there are hard and soft beats. Many poems have the same beat pattern. A hard beat has more force than a soft beat.

> **Jack** and **Jill** went **up** the **hill,**
> To **fetch** a **pail** of **wa**ter;
> **Jack** fell **down** and **broke** his **crown,**
> And **Jill** came **tumb**ling **after.**

Besides figurative language, poets can add *sounds.* This is called **onomatopoeia.** Words that imitate the sound of something, such as *boom, crash,* and *cluck* are examples of onomatopoeia. The poem below uses the phrase *pitter-patter.*

> The rain begins to fall
> On my doorstep,
> pitter-patter.

Writers break up thoughts in paragraphs. Poets may divide lines into **stanzas.** These are groups of lines separated by spaces. The poem that follows is in three stanzas.

Guided Practice

from **Rain in Summer**

by Henry Wadsworth Longfellow

1 How beautiful is the rain!
2 After the dust and heat,
3 In the broad and fiery street,
4 In the narrow lane,
5 How beautiful is the rain!

6 How it <u>clatters</u> along the roofs,
7 Like the tramp of hoofs!
8 How it gushes and struggles out
9 From the throat of the overflowing spout!

10 Across the window-pane
11 It pours and pours;
12 And swift and wide,
13 With a muddy tide,
14 Like a river down <u>the gutter roars</u>
15 The rain, the welcome rain!

Which line in the poem includes a simile?

   A How beautiful is the rain!

   B After the dust and heat,

   C Like the tramp of hoofs

   D The rain, the welcome rain!

Longfellow uses a lot of figurative language in this poem. Yet there is only one simile in your choices. This is "Like the tramp of hoofs." Longfellow is comparing the sound of rain to an animal's hoofs walking on top of a roof. The correct answer is choice C.

In line 3, what is the speaker referring to when he says "fiery street"?

A the heat

B a real fire

C a fire truck

D the heat of the rain

Longfellow wants to show how happy he is for the rain. He wants to express how hot it has been. He uses "fiery" to tell how hot it has been. This helps the reader know how happy everyone is for the rain. There is no fire or fire truck. The rain is not hot. Choice A is the correct answer.

In line 6, the word clatters is an example of _____.

A metaphor

B onomatopoeia

C personification

D literal language

The word clatters carries a sound. The poet wanted you to hear the sound. It is not literal language, personification, or metaphor. We should look for the word that has to do with sound. Onomatopoeia is that word. The correct answer is choice B.

In line 14, the phrase <u>the gutter roars</u> is an example of _____.

A   a simile

B   metaphor

C   personification

D   literal language

We can see a gutter roaring out the rain water. We know the poet is painting word pictures. Literal language is not correct. Nothing is being compared in the underlined phrase. It is not a simile or metaphor. A gutter would not roar. This is an example of personification. The correct answer is choice D.

Idioms

Idioms are also figurative language. An idiom is a phrase. The words have little to do with the actual meaning. For example, you may be afraid to go on stage. A friend may say, *"You have cold feet."* If you never heard the idiom, you are confused. You know your feet are not cold. This is literal thinking. The figurative meaning has nothing to do with *feet that are cold*.

Here are some other familiar idioms:

Idiom	Meaning
cry wolf	to give a false alarm of danger
get your feet wet	try something out for the first time
a green thumb	to have special talents for gardening
hold your horses	slow down, be patient
piece of cake	a very easy task
call it a day	to bring a project to an end
break a leg	good luck in a show

Idioms developed over time. Many times, there is a story behind them. Take the idiom "cry wolf." This started as an Aesop tale. The story was about a boy tending sheep. He would "cry wolf" because he was bored. All the people in town would come. Then they would see his false alarm.

The idiom "break a leg" began in show business. For some reason it was unlucky to wish someone luck. Instead people wished bad luck. If you try to understand idioms word for word, you will be puzzled. Instead, just remember idioms.

What are some other idioms you can think of? Write a few on the lines below.

Idiom	**Meaning**
_____	_____
_____	_____
_____	_____
_____	_____

Guided Practice

Read the passage. Then answer the questions.

White House Water

Before the 1800s, nobody had running water. This made life a little hard. Even the president had no water. Everyone <u>was in the same boat</u>.

In 1801, the president put buckets on the roof. This would collect rain water. This could be used to flush toilets. However, taking baths was another problem. People had to carry water buckets five blocks to the White House. Surely these buckets <u>weighed a ton</u>. They would bring the water into a tub. Then they would heat the water over flames. Heating a tub was like boiling water on a stove. Many times people would just wash in lakes or streams.

In 1829, <u>the ball got rolling</u>. The White House got two well pumps. People had to hand pump the water. At least it was a start. Fifty years later there was running water in the White House. Now, presidents were able to enjoy a hot bath anytime they wanted.

What does the idiom <u>in the same boat</u> mean in this passage?

A had different lives

B had different issues

C had the same problems

D had the same happiness

Look at the context of the paragraph. Nobody had any running water. Therefore, everyone had the same problems. The correct answer is choice C.

The phrase <u>weighed a ton</u> means _____.

A easy

B light

C mean

D heavy

Did the buckets weigh a ton? Probably not. We know this is figurative language. We can also guess it is an idiom. A ton is not light. It is very heavy. Something that weighs a lot is not easy to carry. No person could carry a ton. The correct answer is choice D.

Explain the meaning of the idiom <u>the ball got rolling</u>.

_____

_____

 The last paragraph can help you. It should tell you what this idiom means. Water finally was pumped into the White House. Here is a sample answer:

If the ball gets rolling, it means that something is starting to work well.

Word Connections

Writers use words for many reasons. They can tell about people and things using figurative phrases. Or, writers can also use **literal** words. You may describe your best buddy with literal words. You may say he is friendly and helpful. These kinds of words are useful in everyday life.

You may want to tell a teacher about your new puppy. You want to describe what she is like. You say she is playful and loving. When your puppy grows up, she may change. You may later describe her as brave and sweet.

Guided Practice

Read the story. Then answer the questions.

Piano Blues

Jen did not like the songs that she was forced to play on piano. Her piano teacher was a kind and caring woman, but she always picked out boring music. Jen wanted to play songs she heard on the radio. Jen decided to tell her mother.

"Mom, I do not want to play boring songs anymore."

"I enjoy hearing your songs, Jen," her mom said.

"But I do not. Can you take me to the music store? That way I can get some fun music that I hear on the radio."

"Okay, but I do not think it will sound the way you want it to."

When they returned home, Jen carefully unpacked her new music book. She put it on her piano. Then she began to peck out the notes.

"Mom, this sounds terrible. It does not sound like anything on the radio," Jen said. Jen was almost in tears. She had been hoping this new music would make her happier.

Her mom rushed to her side to calm her. "Let's keep trying out different kinds of music for piano. The radio songs may not sound too great. However, I have some old jazz music that I think you will like."

"Thanks, Mom," Jen said as she hugged her mom tightly.

What words are used to describe Jen's piano teacher? What type of person is she?

_____

_____

_____

✓ **This question asks you to go beyond the literal words. Here is a sample answer:**

Jen's piano teacher is described as kind and caring. We can guess that she is a nice person. She just does not like the same music as Jen.

Why does Jen carefully unpack her new music book?

_____

_____

_____

✓ **Think about what Jen's actions tell you about her feelings. Here's a sample answer:**

Jen thinks that playing new music is a special treat. She shows great care in taking the book out. This shows that she treasures the book.

Why does Jen hug her mom tightly at the end of the story?

_____

_____

_____

✓ Jen's action tells you something about her feelings for her mom.
Here is a sample answer:

Jen's mom has been very patient. Jen is showing how
much her mom means to her. She is showing how much she
loves her.

Comparing Words _____

Synonyms are words that have almost the same meaning.
But there can be a lot of difference in that "almost." Take the
word *smart*. You may like being called smart. However, what if
you were called *brainy?* That may not be so good. Writers have to
be careful while picking out just the right words.

The best way to find synonyms is to look in a **thesaurus.**
A thesaurus is like a dictionary. However, it does not have
definitions. Instead it has synonyms.

Guided Practice

The Scream

Can you hear a painting? Many people think you can. A very <u>famous</u> painting by an artist from Norway makes you hear a scream. Is that possible? Edvard Munch called this painting, *The Scream*.

How does this painting make you feel? Many people say it makes them feel <u>sadness</u>. Others feel <u>uneasy</u> looking at the painting.

There are wavy lines throughout the painting. The man in the front of the picture is holding his ears and screaming. Edvard told how he came about this painting idea. He said he was walking with his friends. All of a sudden nature was crying out to him. He put his hands to his ears to close out the scream of nature. The painting is one he made of himself.

Which word would *best* replace <u>famous</u> in paragraph 1?

   A awful

   B joyful

   C unknown

   D well-known

> We have to try to replace words here. We need to use the context of the passage to help us. The words "awful" and "joyful" are opinions. Most likely the other choices are better. "Well-known" is what we are looking for here. The correct answer is choice D.

Which word is a synonym of <u>sadness</u> in paragraph 2?

    A mad

    B bad

    C grief

    D joy

"Grief" is a synonym for <u>sadness</u> in this context. The other choices mean to be angry, naughty, or happy. They do not make the most sense in context. The correct answer is choice C.

Explain what the word <u>uneasy</u> means in paragraph 2. Give a synonym for it if you can.

_____

_____

_____

Look back to the prefix chart on page 14 to find the meaning of *un-* if you need to.

    <u>Uneasy</u> means that someone does not feel quite right.
    Un- means "not." We know that the word means "not easy."
    Synonyms would be nervous, tense, or troubled.

Issun Boshi: One Inch Boy

Long ago in Japan there was a quiet little village. An old husband and wife always wanted to have children there. However, they were never able to have any. They were feeling down in the dumps. One day they put their heads together and decided to make a wish.

"We wish to have a child. Even if it is no larger than our fingertip, we will love him."

The next day, they had a little baby that was one inch long. They called him Issun Boshi. This means "One-Inch Boy." The boy grew only to the size of his father's thumb. However, he was smart, kind, and helpful.

When Issun Boshi was 12 years old, he was sad. He told his parents that he needed to travel. He wanted to go to the capital, Kyoto. There he wanted to make a name for himself.

His parents felt nervous to let him go. They gave him chopsticks and a rice bowl. With this, he made a boat and paddles. He looked as if he had been a sailor his whole life.

Issun Boshi's rice bowl floated down the river as gentle as a leaf gliding in the wind.

His rice bowl boat stopped at a wealthy man's home.

"Who is there?"

"Me!"

The wealthy man looked down and picked up little Issun Boshi. Just then a fly was buzzing in the man's face. Issun Boshi took out his little sewing needle and was able to spear it. The man was <u>impressed</u>. So he took Issun Boshi into his home.

His daughter, a princess, liked Issun Boshi. They became great friends. One day, the two were at a party. The large Oni monster showed up with his magic hammer. Everyone ran except for the princess and Issun Boshi. The Oni monster took Issun Boshi and popped him into his mouth. <u>Yet, even in the face of danger Issun was brave and daring.</u> He took out his sewing needle and hurt Oni so badly that Oni spit him out. Oni ran away in pain, and forgot his magic hammer.

Issun Boshi made a wish on the magic hammer that he could be taller. His wish came true, and he was just as tall as the princess. Then the wealthy man let Issun Boshi marry his daughter, the princess.

1 The husband and wife felt <u>down in the dumps</u>. The author wants you to understand that they were _____.

   A sad

   B mad

   C excited

   D laughing

2 In the paragraph 1, the husband and wife <u>put their heads together</u>. What does this idiom mean?

   A smile a lot

   B shake their heads

   C look each other in the face

   D think about something deeply

3 In paragraph 3, the author tells about Issun Boshi. What words does the author use? Explain what this says about who Issun Boshi is as a person.

_____

_____

_____

_____

_____

4 In paragraph 5, the author writes, His parents felt nervous to let him go. Explain what the parents were feeling.

_____

_____

_____

_____

_____

5 Read this sentence from the story.

Issun Boshi's rice bowl floated down the river as gentle as a leaf gliding in the wind.

What two things are being compared in this sentence?

A a bowl and the wind

B a bowl and a leaf

C a river and a leaf

D a river and a bowl

6 In paragraph 7, what is another word for <u>wealthy</u>?

    A rich

    B poor

    C broke

    D enough

7 In paragraph 10, the wealthy man is <u>impressed</u> with Issun Boshi. Explain how the wealthy man felt towards the boy.

_____

_____

_____

_____

8 Read this sentence from the story.

Yet, even in the face of danger Issun was brave and daring.

What does <u>in the face of danger</u> mean?

_____

_____

_____

_____

Content-Specific Words

L.3.6, RL.3.4, RI.3.4

You already learned quite a bit about words. Now, you are going to learn about different levels of words. There are four of them.

First, there are the words you use when you talk to your friends. This might include words that even your parents do not understand. Second, you have a polite way of talking to your teachers and parents. You have to be the judge of how you change your language. Third, there are the words used mostly in books or newspapers. Often, these words are powerful and formal. Finally, there are specific words used for different types of reading.

Many subjects have their own words. In science, you use words like *microscope.* In math, you may use words such as *subtract* and *sum.* Social studies uses special words as well. You may read about *capitols.* When reading stories you may discuss words like *character.*

Guided Practice

Read the passage. Then answer the questions.

Moving Sale

It was <u>dreadful</u> enough that we were moving across town, but now Mom wanted to have a moving sale. Mom told me <u>beforehand</u> that we would have to sell some of my toys. Then she took out all my old clothes and toys and started marking prices on them. It was <u>heartbreaking</u> to see how my memories would be sold at twenty-five cents apiece.

"You are selling my dolls, too?" I asked feeling more upset.

"If I saw you playing with them, I would not sell them, but perhaps there may be a little girl who would play with these dolls." Mom <u>hurled</u> the dolls in a brown box, just like that.

I looked down at the ground knowing she was right. Although, it was still hard to let go.

"Please go through your books and let me know which ones you want to keep."

As I proceeded to my room, I looked at my bookcase. I was reading chapter books now, so I did not need to keep my board books. As I picked up my *Baby Beluga* book, the one that mom and I used to dance around and sing to, I just started crying.

"Honey," Mom said as she entered my room. "This is stressful on you, huh?"

"Are you kidding? This is the worst day of my life!"

Mom looked down at the floor. I knew she felt bad, and I didn't want to hurt her feelings. At the same time, I was miserable.

"Tell me what you are feeling," Mom said as she gave me a hug.

"I have to get rid of my dolls, my book, and my toys, and now I have to start a new school and make new friends," I said through my tears.

"You know what? The moving sale can be delayed. This move is putting pressure on both of us, and we need to look forward to this move. We cannot be upset about it, so maybe we can think about something good about our new home."

I stopped crying enough to think something positive. "We have a park nearby, the school is also nicer, and I know I will like my teacher."

"Oh, and your cousin goes to your new school, so that will be a nice treat," Mom added.

"And I get to keep all my toys now, right?" I shouted.

<u>Afterwards</u>, Mom just smiled and hugged me.

The word <u>dreadful</u> in the first sentence of the story means ____.

A ugly

B awful

C perfect

D wonderful

<u>Dreadful</u> is a word that you may or may not use. Look at how it is used in the sentence. The main character does not want to move. "Perfect" and "wonderful" are not good choices here. "Ugly" may be a good choice if she were talking about an object. However, she is talking about the act of moving. The correct answer is choice B.

In the first paragraph, what does the word <u>beforehand</u> mean?

A after

B next

C earlier

D later

<u>Beforehand</u> is a word used to tell about time. Think about the two words that make up this word, "before" and "hand." We can think of a clock hand. Before the hand, something happened. Choices A, B, and D all tell what happens after. The correct answer is choice C.

What is another common word for <u>heartbreaking</u>?

A joyful

B painful

C bothering

D pestering

> When you break someone's heart, you hurt them. The word <u>heartbreaking</u> means almost the same. You have to look for another word that means almost the same. You can probably guess the word means "painful." Choice B is the correct answer.

Write definitions for the other underlined words in the passage. If you can't tell the meaning of the word from the context, look it up in a print or online dictionary.

hurled _____

proceeded _____

miserable _____

delayed _____

afterwards _____

> Did you get them all? Your answers might read something like these:

hurled—threw
proceeded—went on
miserable—unhappy
delayed—late
afterwards—next

John Muir

In 1849, John Muir came to the United States. His Scottish family moved to a home in Wisconsin. John always loved the <u>wilderness</u>. He looked closely at what he found. Then he would write his observations down in his log.

One day he set out on foot. He only had a compass and a small bag of clothes. He walked across our whole country. He spent quite a bit of time on the west coast. He measured Sequoia trees. He <u>estimated</u> one might have been 4,000 years old.

He wrote in a journal about everything he saw. Later he wrote books about his travels. John believed people needed the quiet pleasure found in nature. He wanted to set aside land that could not be destroyed.

He was worried about people cutting down trees. This would <u>damage</u> nature. So he wrote and spoke about <u>preserving</u> nature. His books helped others think about saving forests. Now acres and acres of land are saved as national parks.

In the first paragraph, the word <u>wilderness</u> means _____.

    A open seas

    B nearby cities

    C untouched lands

    D connecting rivers

> <u>Wilderness</u> is a social studies word. We usually use this word when talking about any type of land that is untouched by man. You can figure out the meaning if you do not know it. We know that Muir went to places that other men did not. He traveled far. The correct answer is choice C.

In the second paragraph, the word <u>estimated</u> means ____.

    A facts based on guesses

    B facts that can be measured

    C a lucky guess based on nothing

    D a good guess based on measurements

> ✓ An <u>estimate</u> is good guess based on fact or measurement. It is a math word. John measured the tree. Then he <u>estimated</u> it was 4,000 years old. You have to watch the wording in these answers. The two that have the words *measure* in them are choices B and D. However, facts cannot be measured. Choice D is the correct answer.

In the last paragraph, the word <u>damage</u> is used as a verb. What does it mean to <u>damage</u> something?

_____

> ✓ Think about how the word is used in paragraph 4. Here is a sample answer:

    This means any action that would destroy something.

In the last paragraph we learn about John's work in <u>preserving</u> nature. What does the word <u>preserving</u> mean?

_____

> ✓ Read the next sentence. Think about the context. Here's a sample answer:

    Preserving means saving or putting aside something, like land.

Test Yourself

Algon and the Sky-Girl

an Algonquin Indian legend

Algon was a talented hunter. Once he was hunting alone in the grasslands. He noticed a <u>mysterious</u> circle. He hid in the bushes to see what caused it. Out of the sky dropped a basket of young women. They danced and sang.

As Algon watched, he was amazed. He was fascinated with one of the women, and he wanted to marry her. Every time he tried to get close to her, the girls would run into the basket. Then the basket would float to the sky.

Soon Algon realized he may never have the girl he loves. He had to come up with a plan. He found field mice in the hollow of a tree. He took some magic powder out of his bag. Then he <u>transformed</u> himself into a little mouse.

The next time the girls came down from the heavens, Algon was a mouse. The girls screamed and stomped on the mice. It was just enough time for him to grab the girl he loved. Algon took her to his village, and named her Sky-Girl. The two were married.

<u>In time</u>, Sky-Girl began to love him, and they had a baby. However, Sky-Girl missed her home above the clouds. Every day she sat in the circle waiting for her friends to take her back home. Finally, she made her own basket. She put her baby in it, and they <u>journeyed</u> back to the sky.

Sky-Girl spent many years back in her sky home. Yet, Sky-Girl's child was getting older. He began asking his mom questions. Sky-Girl was also beginning to miss her husband, Algon. <u>After many years</u>, they asked the Sky-Chief to let them go back down to earth. Sky-Chief gave his <u>consent</u>.

UNIT 1 ▓▓▓▓▓▓▓▓▓▓▓▓▓▓▓▓▓▓▓▓▓▓▓▓▓▓▓▓▓▓▓▓▓▓▓▓▓▓▓
Vocabulary Development

Algon was so happy that they returned. He gathered all kinds of gifts to send the Sky-Chief. He took the claw from the bear. He took the feathers from eagles, hawks, and falcons. He took teeth from a raccoon, as well as hide from a deer. He sent all these to the Sky-Chief.

The Sky-Chief was very thankful. He loved all the gifts. And he loved Algon and his daughter. He made the two of them falcons. That way they could soar up to the sky world whenever they wanted to visit him. Then when they wanted to return to earth, they could.

1 In paragraph 1, the word <u>mysterious</u> means almost the same as _____.

   A funny

   B strange

   C unseen

   D normal

2 As used in paragraph 3, <u>transformed</u> means _____.

   A moved

   B walked

   C traded

   D changed

3 In paragraph 4, the phrase <u>in time</u> means *almost* the same as ____.

    A slowly

    B quickly

    C at the start

    D all of a sudden

4 In paragraph 4, which word is *most* like the word <u>journeyed</u>?

    A turned

    B moved

    C walked

    D traveled

5 <u>After many years</u>, as used in paragraph 6, means ____.

    A before

    B quickly

    C as soon as

    D much later

6 What does it mean that the Sky-Chief gave his <u>consent</u> in paragraph 6?

_____

_____

_____

_____

_____

REVIEW

Vocabulary Development

Read the story. Then answer the questions.

Sink or Swim

"Luz, it is your turn."

Coach Jackie smiled directly at me. But I could not grin back. I was sweating bullets. My mom told Coach Jackie that I was scared of water, but they both thought it was a good idea for me to overcome my fear.

I stood at the side of the pool. They were only asking me to jump into about two feet of water.

"Here, Luz. I will hold your hand and you just jump." Coach Jackie was thoughtful, and holding his hand helped.

"Here goes nothing!" I yelled. Following my jump, I noticed the water was only up to my waist. Why was I afraid to jump in? Thankfully, nobody else was around, as they were on the deep side of the pool, the side I dreamed to swim in.

Coach Jackie told me I was doing great, but it was <u>obvious</u> to me that the children on the other end were having much more fun. They were all <u>swimming like tadpoles</u>.

<u>Soon enough</u> the lessons were getting better and better. I was able to float and paddle kick. I still could not move my arms in the water like a windmill, like I saw other swimmers do. But I could manage a good doggy paddle with my hands.

After a few more lessons, <u>it hit me like a ton of bricks</u>. I was not afraid of the water anymore. I knew that I could keep myself afloat in the deep end.

On the last day of classes, I still could not swim like the others. However, I was able to join them on the deep end and feel certain that I would not sink.

1 Which *best* could be used in place of the word <u>overcome</u> in paragraph 2?

  A win

  B suffer

  C rise above

  D fall below

2 <u>I was sweating bullets</u> is an idiom that means _____.

  A wild

  B calm

  C quiet

  D nervous

3 The phrase <u>following my jump</u> in paragraph 6 means _____.

  A after the jump

  B before the jump

  C earlier than the jump

  D rather than the jump

4 The phrase <u>swimming like tadpoles</u> in paragraph 6 describes ____.

    A no swimming

    B weak swimming

    C strong swimming

    D nervous swimming

5 What does the word <u>obvious</u> in paragraph 6 mean?

    A unseen

    B easy to see

    C little known

    D difficult to know

6 The phrase <u>soon enough</u> in paragraph 7 means ____.

    A in time

    B at once

    C keeping up

    D rather than

7 Explain the idiom <u>it hit me like a ton of bricks</u> used in paragraph 8. What did Luz mean?

_____

_____

_____

_____

_____

Going Down Hill on a Bicycle

by Henry Charles Beeching

1 With lifted feet, hands still,
2 I am poised[1], and down the hill
3 Dart, with <u>heedful mind</u>;
4 The air goes by in a wind.

5 Swifter and yet more swift,
6 Till the heart with a mighty lift
7 Makes the <u>lungs laugh</u>, <u>the throat cry</u>:—
8 "O bird, see; see, bird, I fly.

9 "Is this, is this your joy?
10 O bird, then I, though a boy,
11 For a golden moment share
12 Your feathery life in air!"

13 Say, heart, is there aught like this
14 In a world that is full of bliss?
15 'Tis more than skating, bound
16 Steel-shod to the level ground.

17 Speed slackens[2] now, I float
18 Awhile <u>in my airy boat</u>;
19 Till, when the wheels scarce crawl,
20 My feet to the treadles[3] fall.

21 Alas, that the longest hill
22 Must end in a vale[4]; but still,
23 Who climbs with toil[5], wheresoe'er,
24 Shall find wings waiting there.

---

[1]**poised:** calm and ready

[2]**slackens:** slows down

[3]**treadles:** something like pedals that move in circles

[4]**vale:** valley

[5]**toil:** hard work

UNIT 1 ░░░░░░░░░░░░░░░░░░░░░░░░░
Vocabulary Development

8 In line 3, what does it mean to have a <u>heedful mind</u>?

    A careful

    B careless

    C worried

    D nervous

9 Explain the figurative language used in lines 6 and 7.

_____

_____

_____

_____

_____

10 Explain the metaphor used in line 18. What is being compared?

_____

_____

_____

_____

_____

11 Identify the prefix in the word <u>bicycle</u>? What does it mean?

_____

_____

_____

_____

_____

Dogs Know with Noses

Have you ever watched a dog in action? They sniff almost everything. This is how they learn about the world. Studies show that a dog's sense of smell is stronger than ours. It could be 100,000 times stronger. Could you imagine waking up and smelling what every neighbor on your block was cooking for breakfast? Dogs may be able to do just this. In fact, now that we know the strength of a dog's smell, we are beginning to use that power. Dogs are used in airports, schools, and public places. They have found illegal drugs, foods, and even bombs. Dogs also have been used to help learn if a person has cancer.

How does a dog smell? Dogs have wet noses. It is just this place that the dog's strong sense of smell starts. The moist area of the nose catches smells in the air. It then sends the smells to a membrane in the snout that has receiving cells. The messages on these cells are sent to part of the dog's brain. This is the olfactory center, or the smelling center of the brain. A dog's olfactory center is 40 times larger than ours. This is why they are able to smell so much more than we do.

Taking a dog out for a walk is so exciting for these animals. They get to smell all the animals that have passed by, even people. They get to sniff out who has been eating what in the neighborhood. And they get a feeling of where they are living or are visiting through their noses.

12 Which of these meanings *best* fits the word <u>block</u> as it is used in paragraph 1?

   A a cube

   B to stop

   C a piece

   D a street

13 What is the root word of <u>illegal</u>?

   A il

   B gal

   C illeg

   D leg

14 What does the word <u>moist</u> mean in paragraph 2?

   A dry

   B wet

   C cold

   D warm

15 What does the figurative phrase <u>nose catches smells in the</u> <u>air</u> mean in paragraph 2?

_____

_____

_____

_____

16 Paragraph 2 says that messages are sent to the <u>olfactory center</u>. Explain what this center is from information you have read.

_____

_____

_____

_____

UNIT 1 ▨▨▨▨▨▨▨▨▨▨▨▨▨▨▨▨▨▨▨▨▨▨▨▨▨▨▨▨▨▨▨▨▨▨▨▨
Vocabulary Development

Key Ideas and Details

Reading material is all around you! You can find books that have stories, poems, and plays. You read to find out about things you like. Everything you read has ideas and details in them.

This unit is about those ideas and details. As you read, you need to understand big ideas and small details. You need to know which details are important. And you need to know how they connect to one another.

- **In Lesson 4,** you'll learn how to recall details. This will help you remember what a text is about. You will learn how to pick out details. Then you will learn how to join these details with others.

- **Lesson 5** is about big ideas and the details that support them. You will learn how to find the main idea of a text. Knowing the main idea will help you answer, "What did I just read?" You will know how the details support the main idea. Then you can give a summary. This means that you can tell about the most important ideas and details.

- **In Lesson 6,** you will read about stories and plays. You will learn how to find key details about the characters, events, and settings. Then you will learn how they relate with one another to tell a story.

- **Lesson 7** is about how ideas and details connect in nonfiction. People, events, and ideas relate to one another. This helps you better understand what you are reading.

Understanding a Text

RL.3.1, RI.3.1

Vocabulary
moral
publisher
translated

Why do you like your favorite book? You may have noticed that it has many details. Details make a book more fun to read. The details an author uses are important. As you read, focus on **noting and recalling details.** If you do not understand them, you will miss a lot of what the author is telling you. Next time you read, see how many details you know when you finish.

Guided Practice

Read the passage. Then answer the questions.

Roald Dahl was born in Wales on September 13, 1916. His father died when he was only 3. His mother raised him and his five sisters. He was close with his mother. She made him feel good no matter what he had done.

As a young boy, Roald liked to read. His mother told him stories she would make up. He said, "She was a great teller of tales." Even though his father died, Roald had one of his diaries. His father had liked to write. He wrote in it every day.

Find a list of the books Roald Dahl has written on the Internet. Choose one and write a book report about it after you read it.

Like his dad, Roald began a diary when he was 8. He didn't tell anyone about it. He hid it in a box and tied the box to a tree in his yard. He wanted to make sure no one read it. When he wanted to write, he climbed the tree, and sat on a branch.

Roald didn't start writing children's books until the 1960s. He told his children stories at bedtime—that's where the idea for *James and the Giant Peach* came from. *James and the Giant Peach* was his first book. He said that if he had not had his own children, he would not have written children's books. He would not have known what they liked or what kept their interest.

His second book, *Charlie and the Chocolate Factory,* was written in 1964. It was then made into a movie in 1971 and a new version in 2005. Roald believed it was important for kids to enjoy reading. He said, "I have a passion for teaching kids to become readers...."

In his book, *The Witches,* Roald's own mother was the basis for the grandmother. He used the grandmother's character to praise his mother.

Roald died in 1990 when he was 74 years old. His books are still popular today. They have been translated into 34 languages.

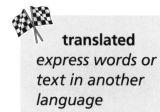

translated
express words or text in another language

In which country was Roald Dahl born?

A France

B Sweden

C Wales

D England

Paragraph 1 gives details about where Roald was born. He was not born in France, Sweden, or England. Choice C is the correct answer.

Who told Roald stories when he was young?

A his father

B his sisters

C his teacher

D his mother

Details give you more information. They are important. Roald will not forget the person who told him stories when he was young. Paragraph 2 tells you choice D is the correct answer.

Where did Roald get the ideas for his stories?

_____

_____

_____

_____

We know that Roald Dahl liked to read and listen to stories growing up. We also know that he liked to write and kept a diary. Paragraph 4 tells us where he got his ideas. Here is a sample answer:

Roald got his ideas from the bedtime stories he told his children. He said that if he had not had children he would not have known what stories they liked. Therefore, he would not have written children's books.

In which section of the library would you find most of Roald Dahl's children's books?

A biography

B fiction

C reference

D history

You know the answer even though none of these words is in the passage. The question asks you to **make an inference.** You must join details that you read with details that you already know. Roald Dahl writes stories about characters that are made up. You know it is fiction. Choice B is the correct answer. The other choices all include facts.

Which character in *The Witches* was like Roald's own mother?

_____

_____

_____

 This detail is in the text. Here is a sample answer:

Roald's mother was like the grandmother in the story, *The Witches*. In paragraph 6, he said he used the character of the grandmother to praise his mom.

Now note details in the story.

Read the passage. Then answer the questions.

The Perfect Gift

"I have to find the perfect gift for Mrs. Burns!" I told my mom.

"Why do you have to get a gift for her?" Mom asked.

"It is her birthday next week. I have been in school for four years, and she is the best teacher I have ever had. I want to get her a really amazing present," I explained.

"Well, James, how much money do you have saved?" Mom inquired.

"I do not know," I thought. "I'll have to count the money in my wallet."

After counting the few dollars I had in my wallet, I was upset. Where had I spent all my money?

"What am I going to be able to buy with $5.50?" I groaned to myself.

"Mom, I only have $5.50," I complained. "I will not find anything. What am I going to do?"

"I know Mrs. Burns will be happy with whatever you get her," Mom said.

"Any gift just will not do," I explained.

"You can do some extra chores around the house," Mom suggested. "That way, you can earn the extra money you need to buy her the gift you want."

"That is a fabulous idea, Mom!" I said. "Can we make a list of all the chores you want completed, and I can get started on them right away?"

I spent the rest of that day and the next working on the list of chores my mom needed done. I cleaned the bathrooms, swept and mopped the floors, and cleaned my room—without just stuffing everything under my bed. After my dad mowed the grass, I raked up the grass clippings. I pulled the weeds that had grown up in the flowerbeds, helped my dad lay wood chips, and then we cleaned the entire garage.

"You have worked really hard today, James," Dad said after we had sat down on the step to drink the lemonade Mom had brought out for us.

"Thanks, Dad," I said.

I was tired and sweaty, but I felt good. I had worked hard, and I was glad I earned the money to buy Mrs. Burns a gift.

"When are you and Mom going shopping?" Dad asked.

"Tomorrow after school," I said.

"What do you think you will get her?" Dad wondered aloud.

"I am going to look for something really special," I said. "I know she is going to be so surprised that I get her a gift, but I want her to know what a great teacher she is!"

"She is lucky to have a wonderful student like you in her class, too, James," Dad said. "Come on, it is time to go in and cool off!"

What is the name of the narrator in the story?

    A   Mom

    B   Dad

    C   James

    D   Mrs. Burns

> In this story, the narrator is one of the characters. You can tell that the narrator isn't Mrs. Burns, Mom, or Dad. The narrator refers to them by name. In the paragraph 4, Mom asks, "Well, James, how much money do you have saved?" The correct answer is choice C.

Why does James want to buy Mrs. Burns a gift?

    A   It is her birthday.

    B   She is getting married.

    C   He wants to say he is sorry.

    D   It is the end of the school year.

> The story begins with James telling his mom that he wants to buy Mrs. Burns the perfect gift. The details tell you that it is Mrs. Burns's birthday. Choice A is the correct answer.

Which of these is *not* a detail that describes James?

A He is in Mrs. Burns's class.

B James keeps his money in his wallet.

C Mrs. Burns is his favorite teacher.

D He is lazy and does not like to work.

The passage tells us that James has a problem. He wants to buy his favorite teacher, Mrs. Burns, a gift. He counts the money in his wallet. However, he does not have enough money to buy the gift he wants. He does extra chores for his mom and dad to get money. We can infer that he is not lazy because he is willing to work. Choice D is the correct answer. It is the only choice that does not describe James.

What are James's parents like? What details in the story give you these clues?

_____

_____

_____

_____

Think about what James's parents say and what they do. Here is a sample answer:

James's mom and dad are nice. They support him. They think he is a good student. They helped him figure out how to earn money. Then his mom was going to take him shopping.

It can be important to note details in advertising, too.

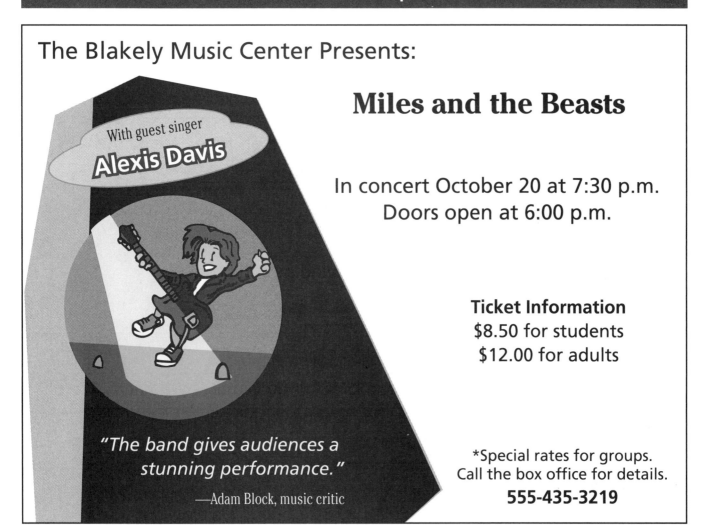

The Blakely Music Center Presents:

Miles and the Beasts

With guest singer
Alexis Davis

In concert October 20 at 7:30 p.m.
Doors open at 6:00 p.m.

Ticket Information
$8.50 for students
$12.00 for adults

*"The band gives audiences a
stunning performance."*
—Adam Block, music critic

*Special rates for groups.
Call the box office for details.
555-435-3219

Who is the featured performer in the concert that is advertised?

A Miles and the Beasts

B Alexis Davis

C Adam Block

D Blakely Music Center

Did you read carefully? Adam Block is quoted in the ad. The concert is being held at the Blakely Music Center. Alexis Davis is a guest singer. The main performer is Miles and the Beasts. Choice A is the correct answer.

Which of these details is *not* included in the ad?

A   ticket prices

B   a website for ordering tickets

C   date of the concert

D   the box office phone number

Ticket prices, the box office phone number, and the date of the concert are all on the poster. A website for ordering tickets is not listed. The correct answer is choice B.

What detail in the ad tells you that you may want to go with a group?

_____

_____

_____

This question asks you about a detail that you have to infer. Here is a sample answer:

The last line of the ad says "Special rates for groups." This means it will cost less if you go with a group of people to see Miles and the Beasts.

Test Yourself

The First African American Poet

Do you know the name of the first female black poet? Her name is Phillis Wheatley. No one knows the date she was born. It is thought to have been sometime in 1753. She was born in Africa. When she was about 8 years old, she was taken and put on a slave ship. The ship was going to America. It was called the *Phillis.* This is how she got her name.

When she got to America, she was sold as a slave. A rich man from Boston named Mr. Wheatley bought her. He wanted Phillis to help his wife. Mr. and Mrs. Wheatley raised Phillis as one of their own children. They wanted her to learn. Phillis learned different languages and studied hard. She wrote her first poem when she was only 13 years old.

Phillis wrote many poems. White people were surprised. They did not think slaves were smart. Many people in Boston liked her writing. She did not become angry or sad when publishers in Boston would not publish her poems. In 1773, the Wheatley's son traveled to London with Phillis to get her poems published. Phillis became the first black writer to get a book published.

Later in October of 1773, she was freed from slavery. Phillis believed everyone should have the choice to be free. Most of Phillis's poems were about moral topics. She even got to read her poetry to George Washington.

In 1784, Phillis died when she was only 31 years old. She is still an inspiration to many people today.

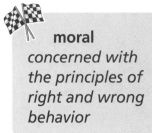

publisher
a person or company that prepares and issues books

Publifhed according to Act of Parliament, Sept.ʳ 1.1773 by Archᵈ Bell, Bookfeller Nᵒ 8 near the Saracens Head Aldgate.

moral
concerned with the principles of right and wrong behavior

1 Phillis Wheatley was born in _____.

   A Africa

   B Boston

   C London

   D America

2 When did the Wheatley's son take Phillis's poems to get published in London?

   A after Phillis had died

   B before they were taken to Boston

   C in the same year as Phillis's death

   D in the same year Phillis became free

3 Who was Mr. Wheatley?

   A the ship captain

   B the man who sold Phillis

   C the man who bought Phillis

   D the man who published Phillis's book

4 White people did not think slaves were _____.

   A clean

   B smart

   C hard workers

   D good musicians

5 How did the Wheatley family help Phillis become a great poet? Use details from the passage to answer this question.

_____

_____

_____

_____

6 Why do you think Phillis wrote poems about moral issues?

_____

_____

_____

_____

Main Idea and Summaries

RL.3.2, RI.3.2

Vocabulary
century
robot
vaccum

Your friend wants to tell you about a book he read. Your first question is, "What is the book about?" He should be able to tell you in only a few sentences.

Any text you read is *about* something. Every text has a **main idea.** Telling someone the main idea means you will answer the question, "What is the book about?" It is an important reading skill. When you know what you are reading *about,* details are clear. The main ideas of part of a text are the details that back up the main ideas of the whole text.

Guided Practice

Read the passage. Then answer the questions.

"A Century of Progress"

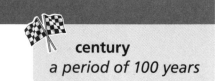

century
a period of 100 years

Chicago's World's Fair was held in 1933 and 1934. At that time, the city of Chicago was 100 years old. It was held to remember its birthday.

The fair was named "A Century of Progress." It was held to show off new science and technology of the time. People came to see new products. They came to see what things were changing. It was held along the shore of Lake Michigan—an easy walk to and from downtown Chicago.

There were many things for the whole family to do at the fair! Parents could walk around and look at the buildings. Children could check out their own area. There were many rides. At Magic Mountain, children could slide down the mountain. They could see a

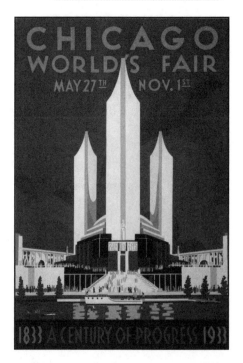

castle. Children could watch a play. There were many games people could play while visiting the fair. There was even a place to watch men wrestle alligators.

Chicago's World's Fair was open for two years. Almost 49 million people visited. It was only planned to be open for one year. Because it was so popular, it was opened for a second year.

Since the fair was held during the Great Depression, we have to wonder if it was a nice break from the hard times.

 Chicago is a city in northeastern Illinois.

Research Chicago's World's Fair. Write about what you would have liked to see at the fair if you had visited.

What is this article *mainly* about?

A   Chicago's World's Fair

B   Magic Mountain

C   Lake Michigan

D   the Great Depression

✓ All these details are in the passage. However, they are not all what the passage is mostly about. The passage is mostly about Chicago's World's Fair. Choice A is the correct answer.

Which sentence *best* expresses the main idea of paragraph 1?

A   It was held to remember its birthday.

B   The fair was named "A Century of Progress."

C   Chicago's World's Fair was held in 1933 and 1934.

D   At that time, the city of Chicago was 100 years old.

✓ In most paragraphs, there is one sentence that tells the main idea. It is called the **topic sentence.** In this paragraph, the first sentence is the topic sentence. The sentences that come after it tell more details about it. Choice C is the correct answer.

What is the topic sentence of paragraph 2?

_____

_____

This paragraph tells readers the name of Chicago's World's Fair. It tells how it got the name. It tells what people would see. Here is a sample answer:

> The fair was called "A Century of Progress." It showed off the new products of the time.

What is the topic sentence of paragraph 3? What details support it?

_____

_____

_____

_____

The topic sentence is not always the first sentence. In this paragraph, the first sentence is the topic sentence. Here is a sample answer:

> The topic sentence is: "There were many things for the whole family to do at the fair." Details that support this are: Parents could walk around and look at the buildings. There were rides, games, and a theater for kids.

Which of these ideas should *not* be in a summary of the passage?

   A The fair was named "A Century of Progress."

   B Chicago's World's Fair was held in 1933 and 1934.

   C It was easy to walk to the fair from downtown Chicago.

   D There were many things for the whole family to do at the fair!

   A **summary** tells the main ideas. It tells the most important details. Choices A, B, and D are all important details. A summary does not need to say that people could walk to the fair from downtown. The correct answer is choice C.

Write a summary of the passage.

_____

_____

_____

_____

   Think about the main idea of each paragraph. Here is a sample response:

       Chicago's World's Fair was held in 1933 and 1934. The fair was named "A Century of Progress." It showed off new science of the time. At the fair, there were things for the whole family to do. There were games, rides, and buildings. It was open for two years. Almost 49 million people came to the fair.

A Monkey and a Crocodile

a fable from India

Monkey and Crocodile were best friends. Monkey lived at the top of a coconut tree near the river, and Crocodile would visit Monkey.

"Hop on top of my back," Crocodile said to Monkey. "I will take you on a relaxing ride around the river. When we are done, I'll return you to your tree."

When Crocodile returned to his home, his wife told him she was sick.

"Someone told me that I will die if I don't eat the liver of a monkey," she told her husband. "Go get a monkey's liver for me. You will save my life if you do."

The next day, Crocodile went to see Monkey.

"My wife would like you to come to our house for dinner. She has prepared something delicious that you will love. Hop on my back, and we will go!" Crocodile said. He was nervous as they swam home, but he saw no other way to help his wife.

While he was swimming along, Crocodile could not keep silent any longer. He told Monkey about why they were really going to his house. Monkey had to think quickly. What should he do to save his life?

"My good friend and companion," Monkey said to Crocodile. "My liver is hanging on my tree. We must go back at once so I can get it."

Crocodile turned around and swam back to Monkey's tree. Immediately, Monkey ran up his tree as high as he could. He did not come back down.

"Where, oh where, are you, Monkey?" Crocodile yelled.

Monkey dropped a coconut right on the top of Crocodile's head.

"Go away!" Monkey screamed. "You are not my friend! Monkeys don't hang their livers in trees. They are inside us!"

What did Monkey ride on in the river?

A   a boat

B   a raft

C   Crocodile

D   a coconut

This asks about a detail in the story. Look at the second paragraph. The story says that Crocodile would take Monkey for a ride on the river on his back. The correct answer is choice C.

Where does Monkey live?

A   at the zoo

B   in the river

C   in a monkey house

D   at the top of a coconut tree

This is another detail in the story. The story tells us, "Monkey lived at the top of a coconut tree near the river." Choice D is the correct answer.

What is the moral of this story? What details support the moral?

_____

_____

_____

_____

_____

 The main idea of a text is sometimes called its **theme.** The theme is different from the plot. The plot tells what happens. The theme is what a text is about. In a fable, the theme is often told as a lesson about life or "moral." Here is a sample answer:

The moral is that true friends do not trick others to get what they want. Crocodile tricked Monkey to get him to come to his house so Crocodile's wife could eat his liver. When Monkey found out, he saved himself by tricking Crocodile. Monkey's quick thinking saved his life.

Which sentence *best* summarizes why Crocodile's wife needed a monkey's liver?

A She was hungry.

B She would die without it.

C She liked to use monkey liver in soup.

D She needed it to save her sick daughter.

 Choice B is the correct answer. The fable says Crocodile's wife told him that she would die if she didn't eat the liver of a monkey. She didn't say that she was hungry or that she wanted to make soup with it. The story does not talk about a daughter.

UNIT 2 ▧▧▧▧▧▧▧▧▧▧▧▧▧▧▧▧▧▧▧▧▧▧▧▧▧▧▧▧▧▧▧▧
Key Ideas and Details

Write a summary of the story.

_____

_____

_____

_____

_____

_____

_____

_____

✔ **Your answer should have only the main events from the story. Here is a sample answer:**

The fable is about a crocodile and monkey that are friends. Monkey rides on Crocodile's back down the river. One day, Crocodile found out his wife was sick. She needed a monkey's liver to get well. She asked Crocodile to get Monkey's liver. Crocodile and his wife made a plan. Crocodile couldn't keep it in any longer, and he told Monkey of the plan to eat his liver. Monkey said his liver was in his tree so Crocodile would bring him back to his tree. Then he could save himself. Monkey ran up the tree and wouldn't come down. When Crocodile wondered where Monkey was, Monkey told him the truth. Monkeys do not hang their livers in their trees. They are in their bodies.

Test Yourself

Domestic Robots: Help You Do Your Chores

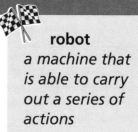

robot
a machine that is able to carry out a series of actions

Stop and think about what life would be like if you had a robot to help do your chores. You would never have to make your bed, dust, or clean your room. You would have a robot to help you do all your chores. Would you like that? Many people are already using robots to help them do their work.

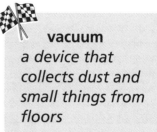

vacuum
a device that collects dust and small things from floors

Roomba is a vacuum cleaner robot. In 2006, over two million Roombas were sold. You can run it when you are at home or when you are gone. It makes vacuuming a snap because it does the work so you do not have to! Can you imagine never having to vacuum again?

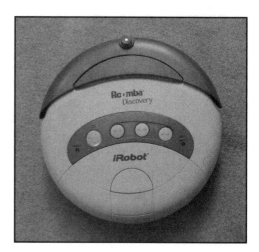

You may know friends that have a pool. Do they vacuum the bottom of their pool? Now there is a robot for that job. What is so nice about them? They do not have hoses. People do not have to hold them. They do not use electricity. You put them in your pool, and they do all the work.

Does your older brother cut the grass in your yard? If he does not enjoy it, a robot lawnmower may be just what he would like. With the push of a button, it will cut grass without having to be pushed around the yard.

In 2010, people have spent more than $17 billion on service and personal robots. Many robots we have today look very much like machines. Most robots only do one job. Robots in the future will look less like machines and will do more than one job.

The robots you see in movies will become more of a reality. They will help us solve problems, do jobs, and help make our lives easier. By 2040, it is thought that most houses will have a personal robot or would like one!

1 What is the main idea of this article?

   A Robots can help us do work.

   B In 2006, over two million Roombas were sold.

   C There is a robot that can clean your pool.

   D If your older brother has to cut the grass, he would like a robot lawnmower.

2 What is the *most* important supporting idea of this article?

   A A Roomba is a vacuum cleaning robot.

   B Many robots we have today look very much like machines.

   C In 2010, people have spent more than $17 billion on service and personal robots.

   D With the push of a button, it will cut grass without having to be pushed around the yard.

3 What is the main idea of paragraph 2?

   A Roomba is a vacuum cleaner robot.

   B In 2006, over two million Roombas were sold.

   C You can run it when you are at home or when you are gone.

   D It makes vacuuming a snap because it does the work so you do not have to!

4 Which of these would make the *best* heading for paragraph 6?

   A Roomba

   B Robots of the Future

   C Pool Robots

   D A Robot for the Yard

5 Write a sentence that expresses the main idea of paragraph 1.

_____

_____

_____

_____

6 Write a summary of the article.

_____

_____

_____

_____

Literary Elements

RL.3.3

What do you like about fiction? Is it the **characters,** the people in the story? Maybe it is the **plot,** the order of **events** in the story. Is it the **setting?** The setting is when and where the story takes place.

All these things make up a good story. The characters and the ways they think, feel, and act help move the plot along. The plot is the **conflict** or problem that makes the story exciting. The setting helps make the characters and determines what they do.

A story may be realistic fiction, a myth or folktale, a fantasy, or a tale set in the past. It can even be told in a poem. No matter how the story is told, it will always include characters, plot, and setting.

Analyzing a Character

The chart below can help you know more about a character. As you read, fill it in with what you learn. Then you can use what you learn about him to better understand why he did what he did. You will also learn how he relates to the plot.

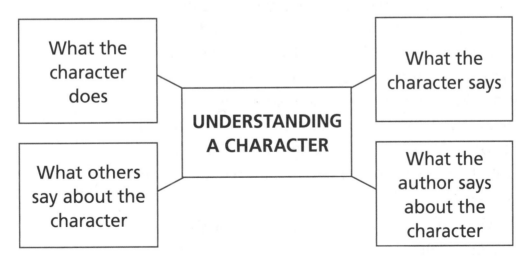

© The Continental Press, Inc.   DUPLICATING THIS MATERIAL IS ILLEGAL.

Guided Practice

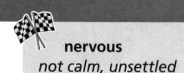

nervous
not calm, unsettled

Career Day

I had been worrying about Career Day all month since my teacher announced it to the class last month. Our parents had signed up at the Open House to speak to the class about their jobs. Now that the day was almost here, I was even more nervous.

What is the point of Career Day, anyway? I thought to myself. *For parents to brag about what they do? What if I don't want my dad to tell what he does? Do I not have a say in whether or not my dad comes to speak?*

Mom could tell something was wrong at dinner. I'm sure the way I was hanging my head and pushing around the spaghetti and meatballs, my favorite dinner, on my plate was noticeable.

"What is wrong, Billy?" Mom asked.

"Oh, nothing that you can fix, Mom," I said. "I do not really want Dad to come to talk to my class tomorrow for Career Day."

"Why not?" Mom seemed confused. "Your dad works hard. He loves you. Your classmates should get to see that."

I dropped it because I did not want my mom to be mad at me. Dad worked two jobs. No one else's dad in my class had to work two jobs. Everyone else's dad was a boss or owned his own company. They had interesting careers to tell us about. Matt's dad bought and sold businesses. Katie's mom and dad were both doctors. Hannah's dad was a dentist. He brought us all toothbrushes and flossing kits when he visited the class. The other careers we heard about swirled in my head.

"I will never make any friends this year," I thought, as I lay in bed trying to fall asleep.

I walked into my classroom with a knot in my stomach. To my surprise, my dad was already at the front of the room. I gave him a quick wave and nervous smile as I took my seat. Maybe there would be a lot of kids missing from school today.

"Boys and girls," my teacher began, "This is Mr. Bradley, Billy's dad. Please welcome him to our class. He is going to tell us about being a firefighter and his part-time job as a pizza delivery man. He has also brought you a special treat for lunch—pizza!"

When the class heard pizza, they let out screams and hollers of praise. Boys around me were giving me high fives and pats on my back.

"Your dad is awesome! He has such a cool job!" Matt said to me across the aisle.

"Can I come to your house for dinner?" Kyle spoke from behind me.

I smiled up at my dad feeling sad for being ashamed that he had two jobs. I knew he worked hard for our family. It should not matter that he has to work two jobs. I should appreciate that he takes care of us so well!

Which of these *best* describes Billy?

A a bully

B happy

C ashamed

D class clown

We know from Billy's actions that he is not a bully, happy, or the class clown. The story tells us that Billy was "sad for being ashamed." He didn't want his classmates to find out his dad had two jobs. Choice C is the correct answer.

Which of these *best* describes Billy's dad?

A mean

B funny

C hard-working

D careless about family

We can understand more about Billy's dad if we think about what we read about him in the story. Look back to see what Billy's mom says about him. She says, "Your dad works hard. He loves you. Your classmates should get to see that." Choice C is the correct answer.

UNIT 2
Key Ideas and Details

Describe Billy as the main character in the story, as well as the plot and setting.

_____

_____

_____

_____

_____

_____

_____

_____

✓ **Think about where the events take place. What happened first? Next? Here is a sample answer:**

Billy is nervous about Career Day. He does not want his dad to talk to his class. His classmates' parents all have neat jobs. They were doctors, dentists, and owners and bosses of companies. Billy thought that when they found out his dad had two jobs, they would make fun of him. He was worried he would not have any friends. Billy's mom reminded him that his dad works hard. When the class learns that Billy's dad brought pizza for the class, they are excited. They think Billy has a cool dad. In the end, Billy feels bad for feeling ashamed about his dad.

At the end of the story, how do you know that Billy does not have to worry about what his dad does? Explain your reasons.

_____

_____

_____

_____

_____

 Think about what Billy's classmates say and do. Here is a sample answer:

When the class finds out that Billy's dad brought pizza for them they scream and shout because they are so happy. Matt tells Billy his dad is "awesome" and has "a cool job." Kyle asks if he can come over for dinner. His classmates do not care that his dad has two jobs.

Elements of Drama

Dramatic literature is written to be performed by actors. It tells a story. It uses special elements that give instructions to directors and actors to make the story exciting.

A **play** is a story that is acted out. A play is usually divided into **acts** and **scenes.**

A list of the **characters** is called the **cast.** They perform the play's action. The list of the cast is at the beginning of the play.

The **setting** is when and where the story takes place. Sometimes, the narrator tells about the setting. Other times, you know the setting by looking at the things on the stage.

Dialogue is the words the characters say. In a **script,** dialogue comes after the character's name.

Stage directions tell actors how to move around the stage and talk.

Props are things that are used on stage. They are things like a bike or backpack. **Scenery** is the backgrounds and larger props that create the setting. **Lighting** refers to the types of lights used on stage. The props, scenery, and lighting are usually described in the stage directions.

Guided Practice

Read the play. Then answer the questions.

The Monkey and the Crocodile

a one-act play

Characters:

Monkey

Crocodile

Crocodile's Wife

Narrator

Scene 1

A jungle with many trees, bushes, and lush flowering plants. A coconut tree is in the middle of the jungle. A flowing blue river winds through the jungle.

NARRATOR: Monkey and Crocodile were best friends. Monkey lived at the top of a coconut tree near the river, and Crocodile would visit Monkey almost every day. One of their favorite things to do together was riding through the river. Monkey would ride on Crocodile's back as they made their way around the river.

CROCODILE: Come down, Monkey, it is a beautiful day! Hop on my back. I will take you on a relaxing ride around the river. When we are done, I'll return you to your tree.

MONKEY: My, it is such a lovely day for a ride. Thank you for asking me! *(Monkey uses a long stick as a paddle as he sits on Crocodile's back.)*

NARRATOR: Monkey and Crocodile spent most of the day on the river. They talked about what was happening in their neighborhoods and their families. When the day was coming to an end, Crocodile returned Monkey to his tree.

MONKEY: Thanks for the ride, my good friend! See you soon!

CROCODILE: Anytime!

NARRATOR: When Crocodile got home, his wife was waiting for him.

CROCODILE'S WIFE (looking annoyed): Where have you been all day? I've been waiting and waiting.

CROCODILE: I told you I was going for a ride along the river with Monkey.

CROCODILE'S WIFE: I know, I know. I just expected you back hours ago. We have a big problem. I am very sick. Someone told me that I would die if I don't eat the liver of a monkey. Go get your friend Monkey's liver for me. You will save my life if you do.

NARRATOR: Crocodile did not know what to do. He spent many hours into the night trying to decide if he could hurt his friend to save his wife.

Scene 2

The middle of the river. Water is flowing rapidly around Crocodile and Monkey as they ride down the river. The sun is shining high in the sky. It is a hot day. Birds are heard chirping and calling to one another in the jungle.

MONKEY (smiling as he lifts his face to the sun): Thanks again for inviting me for dinner. I know your wife has made something delicious.

CROCODILE (looking nervous): Oh, Monkey! I cannot take it any longer! I must tell you why I have invited you for dinner. My wife is sick and she will get well if she eats a monkey's liver.

MONKEY (looking frantic): What? That is so sad! But wait, my liver is hanging on my tree. We must turn around so I can go get it.

CROCODILE: Thank you, dear friend!

NARRATOR: Crocodile swam quickly back to Monkey's tree. When they were on the riverbank, Monkey took off and ran up to the topmost branch of his tree. He waited without making a sound.

CROCODILE: Where, oh where, are you, Monkey? I am waiting for you.

MONKEY (*dropping a coconut right on the top of Crocodile's head*): Go away! You are not my friend! Monkeys don't hang their livers in trees. They are inside us!

Which of these lines is an example of dialogue spoken by Monkey?

A MONKEY:

B Thanks for the ride, my good friend! See you soon!

C *(looking annoyed)*

D Where, oh where, are you, Monkey?

You noticed that *italic* type is used for directions (choice C). Regular type is used to show lines that are spoken (choices B and D). CAPITALS are used for the names of characters (choice A). Choice D is dialogue spoken by Crocodile. The correct answer is choice B.

What is an example of a prop used in this play?

_____

A prop is an object that is easily moved and used by an actor. You wouldn't consider a tree or the river a prop. Here is a sample answer:

An example of a prop is a long stick used as a paddle.

Which of these sentences *best* describes the dialogue between Monkey and Crocodile at the beginning of the play?

   A   Monkey and Crocodile are best friends.

   B   Monkey and Crocodile do not get along.

   C   Monkey and Crocodile fight when they are together.

   D   Monkey and Crocodile do not like to do the same things.

> We can see from the dialogue that Monkey and Crocodile do get along. They ride along the river together. They do not fight. They seem to like the same things because they spend so much time together. The correct answer is choice A. The narrator tells us they are best friends at the beginning of the play.

Read the lines of this excerpt.

> MONKEY *(smiling as he lifts his face to the sun):* Thanks again for inviting me for dinner. I know your wife has made something delicious.

What do the stage directions tell you?

   A   Monkey cries as he speaks.

   B   Monkey speaks with excitement.

   C   Monkey looks down at the river.

   D   Monkey smiles up at the sun.

> The directions tell the actor playing Monkey how he should act when he speaks. The directions say Monkey should be *"smiling as he lifts his face to the sun."* The correct answer is choice D.

Contrast the settings of the two scenes in this excerpt. How do they appear to an audience?

_____

_____

_____

✓ **Think about what the two friends are doing. Where are they? Here is a sample answer:**

> The first scene begins in the jungle near Monkey's tree. Then they go for a ride on the river. The second scene begins on the river and ends at Monkey's tree.

Read the story "Monkey and the Crocodile" on pages 74–75. Use the play and the story to answer the question.

How is the story different than this play? How are they the same?

_____

_____

_____

✓ **Think about what is the same. Then think about what is different. Here is a sample answer:**

> The story is not broken into two parts. The play has two parts. The play tells who is speaking. They both tell the same story. The characters are the same, too.

Test Yourself

excavating
digging

Oh my Darling, Clementine

by Percy Montrose

1   In a cavern, in a canyon,
2   Excavating for a mine,
3   Dwelt a miner, forty-niner
4   And his daughter–Clementine.

CHORUS:

5   Oh my Darling, Oh my Darling,
6   Oh my Darling Clementine.
7   Thou art lost and gone forever,
8   Dreadful sorry, Clementine.

9   Drove she ducklings to the water
10 Every morning just at nine,
11 Hit her foot against a splinter
12 Fell into the foaming brine.

13 Ruby lips above the water,
14 Blowing bubbles soft and fine,
15 But alas, I was no swimmer,
16 So I lost my Clementine.

17 How I missed her! How I missed her!
18 How I missed my Clementine,
19 But I kissed her little sister,
20 And forgot my Clementine.

1 The speaker, or main character, in this poem is most likely _____.

   A the father of Clementine

   B the mother of Clementine

   C the boyfriend of Clementine

   D the best friend of Clementine

2 What is the speaker sad about?

   A He cannot swim.

   B He cannot find gold.

   C Clementine drowned.

   D Clementine lost her shoes.

3 How does the speaker feel about Clementine? Explain your answer.

_____

_____

_____

_____

4 What kind of work did Clementine's father do?

_____

_____

_____

_____

5 Read this stanza from the poem:

> *Drove she ducklings to the water*
> *Every morning just at nine,*
> *Hit her foot against a splinter*
> *Fell into the foaming brine.*

What does this tell you about Clementine?

_____

_____

_____

_____

_____

UNIT 2 ▚▚▚▚▚▚▚▚▚▚▚▚▚▚▚▚▚▚▚▚▚▚▚▚▚▚▚▚▚
Key Ideas and Details

Analyzing Events and Concepts

RI.3.3

Vocabulary
cacao
calculated
discrimination
lawyer

People, events, and ideas all relate to each other. When you read, you have to think about these relationships. This helps you better understand what you read.

As you read, think about how events flow. Events flow from one to the next. Events relate to each other. The order in which events happen is called **sequence.** Whether you are reading about someone's life or how to do something, there is a sequence of events to follow. Look for clue words that show the sequence. These are words like *first, second, next, before, following, finally, now, after,* and *then.*

You may also want help understanding why things happen. You can ask yourself, "Why did that happen?" That is the **cause.** Then ask, "What happened?" This is the **effect.** Look for clue words that signal **causes:** *if, because, since, due to.* These clue words signal **effects:** *then, so, as a result of, that is why.*

Guided Practice

Read the passage. Then answer the questions.

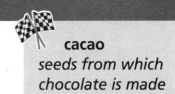

cacao
seeds from which chocolate is made

The History of Chocolate

by Stacy Rummel

When was the last time you ate a chocolate chip cookie? Did you stop to think how we get chocolate or where it comes from?

Over 2,000 years ago, the people of Mexico and Central America found the cacao tree. It was growing in the rainforest. The tree had pods. The seeds in the pods were crushed and made into chocolate.

Mayan people planted the tree in their own yards. They mashed the seeds using a stone. They mixed the seeds with spices to make a drink. They sold the seeds to Aztec traders. They liked the drink, but they could not grow the trees.

Later, cacao seeds were also used as money. While shopping, people could pay for the food, clothes, and items they bought at the market with cacao seeds. Some people tried to trick others by making fake cacao seeds.

The Spanish came to Central America and Mexico in 1500s. They brought cacao seeds back to Spain with them. They made new recipes. After a while, the favorite drink spread across Europe and the rest of the world.

Where do cacao trees grow best? They grow in the shade below taller trees of the rainforest. Cacao trees have flowers on them. They do not produce fruit until they are 3 to 5 years old.

How many seeds come from one cacao pod? There are between 30 and 50 seeds that come from one pod. The seeds are the size of an almond. The seeds from one pod can make about seven candy bars.

The next time you eat a piece of chocolate, think about how people used it long ago!

According to the passage, which of these events happened *first?*

A Cacao seeds were used as money.

B The Spanish brought cacao seeds back to Spain.

C The drink spread to Europe and around the world.

D People found the cacao tree growing in the rainforest.

Knowing the order of events is important. You can use the dates to help you. You can use words like *later* or *after that.* Look back at the text. Choice D is the correct answer. People find the cacao tree before the other events.

How did the Mayans use the cacao seeds to make a drink?

_____

_____

✓ **The passage tells us the steps the Mayans followed. Here is a sample answer:**

> The Mayans mashed the cacao seeds using a stone.
> Then they mixed the seeds with spices to make a drink.

Why were cacao seeds used as money?

_____

_____

_____

✓ **To answer this question, think about what you know about money. Put that together with what you learn in the text. Here is a sample answer:**

> Many people liked cacao seeds. They made a popular
> drink. People could pay for the things they bought with the
> seeds because they were worth something and well liked.
> It was almost like a trade.

Chocolate Chip Cookies

$2\frac{1}{4}$ cups all-purpose flour

1 teaspoon baking soda

1 teaspoon salt

1 cup (2 sticks) butter, softened

$\frac{3}{4}$ cup white sugar

$\frac{3}{4}$ cup packed brown sugar

1 teaspoon vanilla extract

2 large eggs

2 cups (12-ounce package) chocolate chips

1. Preheat oven to 375° F.

2. Put flour, baking soda, and salt in a small bowl. Set aside.

3. Beat butter, both sugars, and vanilla in a large mixer bowl until creamy. Add eggs, one at a time, beating well each time you add an egg.

4. Slowly beat in flour mixture. Stir in chocolate chips.

5. Put rounded tablespoons of dough on ungreased baking sheets.

6. Bake for 9 to 11 minutes or until golden brown. Cool on baking sheets for 2 minutes. Remove and put on wire racks to cool completely.

Which of these steps do you do *first?*

A Combine flour and baking soda.

B Beat butter and sugars.

C Preheat oven to 375° F.

D Slowly beat in flour mixture.

You must follow steps when you bake. Each step has a relationship to the next. If you miss a step or do them out of order, you could end up with food that isn't good. Choices A, B, and D are all steps that come *after* preheat the oven. Choice C is the correct answer.

Which of these steps do you do *before* you add the eggs?

A Stir in chocolate chips.

B Slowly beat in flour mixture.

C Bake for 9 to 11 minutes.

D Beat butter and sugars.

This question asks you to follow steps in order. Choice D is the correct answer.

What could happen if you didn't do step 1?

_____

_____

This question asks you to **make a prediction.** When you bake cookies, you use an oven. Here is a sample answer:

The cookies would be ready to bake. However, the oven would not be hot. You would have to wait for the oven to heat up to bake the cookies.

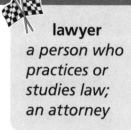

Jane Bolin: First African American United States Judge

Jane Bolin was born in New York on April 11, 1908. Her father was a lawyer. After school, Jane liked to spend time at his office. She liked the books he had in his office. Jane knew she would be a lawyer one day.

In 1928, Jane graduated from Wellesley College. There was only one other black student in her class. After college, Jane went to Yale University. There were only two other women in her class. Jane was the only black woman. While at both schools, she was treated differently because she was black. She had a hard time making friends. Jane spent a lot of time by herself.

Jane was interested in helping people that were poor. She did not like the racial discrimination she and other African Americans faced every day. Even at a young age, Jane wanted to solve social problems like these.

She was a hard worker. Until she passed the New York State bar in 1932, she worked at her father's law office. She married another lawyer. In 1937, they opened their own law office in New York City. Then in 1939, she became a family court judge. Jane was the first black judge. She was a judge for 40 years.

discrimination
unjust treatment because of race, age, or gender

Jane had one son. Her husband died when her son was only 2 years old. Jane became a single mom and judge. She worked hard to spend time with her son and work as a judge. Jane has said, "I didn't get all the sleep I needed, and I didn't get to travel as much as I would have liked, because I felt my first obligation was to my child." Jane got married again in 1950.

Jane Bolin's story should inspire all of us to work hard to make our dreams come true!

Identify which of these events happened *first.*

   A Jane went to Yale University after college.

   B In 1939, she became a family court judge.

   C She passed the New York State bar in 1932.

   D In 1928, Jane graduated from Wellesley College.

> The events in the passage are in order of how they occurred. Think about the order in which the events were written. Use the dates included in the passage to help. The correct answer is choice D.

Why did Jane want to become a lawyer?

_____

_____

_____

> This question asks you to find a reason something happened— to find **cause and effect.** The effect was that Jane wanted to become a lawyer. A detail in the text tells the cause. Here is a sample answer:

> Jane's father was a lawyer. She liked to visit his office after school. She liked the books he had in his office. Jane wanted to become a lawyer when she grew up.

Why did Jane spend a lot of time by herself in college?

A She spent time at her father's law office.

B People treated her differently because she was black.

C She was busy taking care of her husband, son, and their home.

D She had a lot of homework to do and little time to spend with others.

You are asked to identify a cause. The effect was that Jane spent a lot of time by herself. You can look back in the text to read why she spent time by herself. The text says, "While at both schools, she was treated differently because she was black. She had a hard time making friends. Jane spent a lot of time by herself." Choice B is the correct answer.

According to the article, how did Jane overcome discrimination?

_____

_____

_____

_____

Here you need to think about the whole article. How did discrimination affect Jane? Here is a sample answer:

Jane was one of two black students in college. At Yale, there were only two other girls in her class. She was the only one that was black. When she became a judge, she was the first black judge. She did not let people tell her that because she was black she could not follow her dream.

Test Yourself

calculated
to determine

Earthquake!

Have you felt an earthquake? An earthquake is the sudden shaking of the ground. They happen along fault lines of Earth's crust. Scientists cannot tell when an earthquake will happen. They are working to be able to in the future.

The power of an earthquake can be calculated. Some earthquakes are felt more than others. You may see hanging pictures move or hear items on shelves rattle during an earthquake. The Richter scale measures earthquakes. An earthquake that is less than 4.0 does not usually break things. Those that are less than 2.0 cannot be felt. An earthquake that is 7.0 is a big earthquake. Earthquakes usually last less than one minute.

If there is an earthquake, there are a few things you should do. You should drop, cover, and hold. Get down on the ground. Cover yourself with something that will protect you, like the kitchen table. Hold on to it until the shaking stops. Make sure to stay away from windows. If you are outside, get away from buildings, streetlights, and poles. The most important thing to do is to stay calm.

There may be after shocks after the earthquake. These are smaller earthquakes that can cause more damage.

In 1906, there was an earthquake that measured 6.7 on the Richter scale. It happened in San Francisco, California. Someone that experienced it said, "It was like riding a bicycle down a long flight of stairs."

1 Which of these is the *first* thing you should do if there is an earthquake?

A Get down on the ground.

B Hold on until the shaking stops.

C Turn off all the lights in the house.

D Cover yourself with something that will protect you.

2 An earthquake happens along _____.

A holes

B fault lines

C narrow streets

D buildings that line the street

3 The *most* important thing to do during an earthquake is _____.

A stay calm

B stay near windows

C go outside to see what is happening

D call your mom to make sure she is fine

4 What happens during an earthquake?

_____

_____

_____

_____

_____

5 What is used to measure earthquakes?

_____

_____

_____

_____

_____

REVIEW

Key Ideas and Details

Read the passage. Then answer the questions.

The Rabbit and the Elephant

a retelling of an Indian fable

An enormous herd of elephants lived in a forest in India. Men had begun to chop down trees in their forest. The elephants that lived there were confused and scared. The lake they had gotten water from for many years was drying up. They would surely die if they did not move. They decided to begin a search for a new home in the forest.

The new home the elephants traveled to was the home of many rabbits. When the elephants moved in, they destroyed the rabbits' homes with their large feet. They stepped on some of the rabbits, and they were hurt or killed. The rabbits knew something had to be done quickly.

That night, they called a meeting.

"The elephants are not trying to harm us," Long Ears said. "But we cannot live here with them. They are giant creatures."

"How can we get them to leave?" asked a rabbit.

"We have to have a grand plan," said Long Ears. "We are not stronger than them so we cannot fight. We must think smart to win."

"Please go to the elephants and talk to them," another rabbit said.

The following night, Long Ears went to speak to Elephant King. Elephant King was surprised the tiny creature had come to see him.

"My name is Long Ears. I have been sent by the king of the rabbits. My king, the Moon, asks that you take your herd to another lake. He does not want other animals on his land," Long Ears said.

"Please take me to your king, the Moon," Elephant King replied.

"The Moon is in the lake. You can see him if you go look, but he does not want to be bothered," Long Ears said as he pointed to the reflection of the Moon in the lake.

Elephant King could see that the Moon was a mighty ruler. He did not want to disobey his orders. The herd left in the morning.

"Using the names of those with greatness can accomplish many things!" Long Ears said.

1 Which is the *best* moral for this story?

A Size is everything.

B A smart plan can defeat the strong.

C Only the strong survive.

D Don't ask anyone else to solve your problems for you.

2 Long Ears becomes _____.

    A the smallest rabbit

    B the king of the elephants

    C the speaker for the rabbits

    D sad when the elephants win

3 What is the main idea of paragraph 2?

    A The elephants had large feet.

    B The elephants destroyed the rabbits' homes.

    C The elephants were looking for a new home.

    D There were many rabbits in the elephants' new home.

4 Why did Long Ears say, "We have to have a grand plan"?

    A There was not enough water for them and the elephants at the lake.

    B They had many rabbits to feed and not enough food for the elephants.

    C They could not win a fight against the elephants because they were too small.

    D He wanted to show the elephants that the forest was a great place to call home.

5 Long Ears' rabbit friends lived in _____.

    A the jungle

    B the forest

    C a village

    D a large city

6 Explain why this story may have been written.

    A to give a reader new information

    B to help students learn about the moon

    C to explain an important lesson

    D to tell about elephants and rabbits

7 Identify which detail does *not* belong in a summary of the story.

    A The new home the elephants traveled to was the home of many rabbits.

    B The elephants were confused and scared when men chopped down their forest.

    C Long Ears went to see Elephant King to convince him and his herd to leave the forest.

    D When Elephant King asked who was the king of the rabbits, Long Ears said, "the Moon."

8 We know that the rabbits are smart because ____.

    A the narrator tells us

    B they speak to the elephants

    C they do not beat the elephants but have a good plan

    D they overpower the elephants even though they are much smaller

9 How do the rabbits defeat the elephants?

_____

_____

_____

_____

_____

Chloe Helps Those in Need

legacy
something that happened in the past that is passed on

Chloe Sawma grew up in a suburb of Chicago. She could have been your next-door neighbor. Chloe was a sweet and lively fourth grader. She was like many of your friends. The only difference was that Chloe had brain cancer.

Even while she was going to the hospital for treatments, she packed a lunch for a homeless man she saw on her way. She wanted to show others what it meant to love and give. Her goal was always to make others smile.

When Chloe was no longer able to walk, she still thought of others. One girl she met at the hospital was very sick. Chloe wanted to brighten her day. She gave the girl a gift, smiled at her, and said, "I know how you feel."

Chloe seemed to understand how others felt. People were surprised that a child so young could know these things. While staying at the Ronald McDonald House, Chloe worked to make sure the kids around her were happy. While playing games and doing activities, she helped others join in. If what Chloe tried to get the kids involved did not work the first time, she kept on trying. She wanted their sadness to be turned into happiness.

Chloe lost her battle to brain cancer in 2010. But her legacy continues. "Chloe's Crew" is an organization that began to continue the work that Chloe did. Chloe's Crew meets the needs of people through "random acts of love and kindness." It provides school supplies, clothes, and meals for those in need. It also supports brain cancer research.

How does Chloe's story inspire you to help those around you?

UNIT 2 ▓▓▓▓▓▓▓▓▓▓▓▓▓▓▓▓▓▓▓▓▓▓▓▓▓▓▓▓▓▓▓▓▓▓▓▓
Key Ideas and Details

10 According to the author, how did Chloe help others?

_____

_____

_____

_____

_____

11 Chloe's Crew began to ____.

A keep kids in school

B help kids with brain cancer

C feed the homeless in the suburbs

D continue the work Chloe had started

12 Which of these is the topic sentence of paragraph 2?

A She packed a lunch for a homeless man.

B Her goal was always to make others smile.

C She was going to the hospital for treatments.

D Chloe was a sweet and lively fourth grader.

13 Chloe grew up in ____.

A Rockford

B Chicago

C a suburb of Chicago

D the Ronald McDonald House

14 What was the *main* reason Chloe tried to get kids involved in games at the Ronald McDonald House?

    A She wanted to beat them.

    B There were not enough players without them.

    C She wanted their sadness to be turned into happiness.

    D It was her job to make sure others joined in the games.

15 Chloe's Crew began ____.

    A before Chloe was in third grade

    B after Chloe lost her battle to brain cancer

    C before Chloe lost her battle to brain cancer

    D after Chloe asked her parents for permission

16 You can predict that Chloe's Crew ____.

    A will teach people to read

    B will not help many people

    C will not inspire other in the world

    D will help bring smiles to many people

17 Write a summary of the passage. Include only the main ideas and most important details.

_____

_____

_____

_____

_____

Writing is a little like building something. Writers think about why they are writing. They think about who will read it. Writers carefully choose words. They put words into sentences. Then they put sentences into paragraphs. Writers put paragraphs together to build something bigger.

- **In Lesson 8,** you will learn how writers build stories, poems, songs, and plays. You will learn that stories are made of sentences, paragraphs, and chapters. Then you will learn that poems are made of lines and stanzas. You will learn that scenes fit together to build plays. You will see how writers tell stories. You will see how a character grows and learns.

- **Lesson 9** is about writing that tells facts and gives ideas. This kind of writing is in textbooks, magazines, and web pages. Writers may use text features to make it easier for readers to read and understand the text. Some of these are key words, hyperlinks, and text boxes.

- **Lesson 10** is about point of view. In this lesson, you will learn how to recognize the author's point of view. *How* a story or facts are told depends on the author's purpose. It depends on what the author wants to tell. The writer's point of view can shape the way you read. It can shape the way you understand.

Literary Structure

RL.3.5

Vocabulary

bough
bundles
hosts
pinching
plumed
ruddy
russet
scorched
sorrow
swallows
tend
thrushes
wheatsack

Do you pay attention to text structure when you read? All text has structure. A book has paragraphs and chapters. A play has acts and scenes. A poem has lines and stanzas. Each piece of text builds on another. Many times authors write a book, play, or poem in sequence. Putting ideas or events in order helps you build meaning.

Guided Practice

Read the poem. Then answer the questions.

Robin Redbreast

William Allinghamn

1   Goodbye, goodbye to Summer!
2   For Summer's nearly done;
3   The garden smiling faintly,
4   Cool breezes in the sun;
5   Our Thrushes[1] now are silent,
6   Our Swallows[2] flown away
7   But Robin's here, in coat of brown,
8   With ruddy[3] breast-knot gay.
9   Robin, Robin Redbreast,
10 O Robin dear!
11 Robin singing sweetly
12 In the falling of the year.

---

[1]**thrushes:** family of songbirds, including robins
[2]**swallows:** small, fast-flying birds
[3]**ruddy:** healthy, red color

13 Bright yellow, red, and orange,

14 The leaves come down in hosts[4];

15 The trees are Indian Princes,

16 But soon they'll turn to Ghosts;

17 The leathery pears and apples

18 Hang russet[5] on the bough[6],

19 It's Autumn, Autumn, Autumn late,

20 'Twill soon be winter now.

21 Robin, Robin Redbreast,

22 O Robin dear!

23 And what will this poor Robin do?

24 For pinching[7] days are near.

25 The fireside for the Cricket,

26 The wheatsack[8] for the Mouse,

27 When trembling night-winds whistle

28 And moan all round the house;

29 The frosty ways like iron,

30 The branches plumed[9] with snow–

31 Alas! In Winter, dead, and dark,

32 Where can poor Robin go?

33 Robin, Robin Redbreast,

34 O Robin dear!

35 And a crumb of bread for Robin,

36 His little heart to cheer.

With the group, use the Internet to find "When the Red, Red Robin Comes Bob-Bob-Bobbing Along," a song and lyrics by Harry Woods written in 1926. Sing the song together. What does the song say about robins? How does the song make you feel?

---

[4]**hosts:** many

[5]**russet:** reddish-brown color

[6]**bough:** tree branch

[7]**pinching:** painfully cold

[8]**wheatsack:** bag of grain

[9]**plumed:** covered in

UNIT 3
Craft and Structure

115

How many lines are in each stanza of the poem?

A three

B four

C eight

D twelve

There are twelve lines in each stanza. The correct answer is choice D.

How many stanzas are in this poem?

A one

B two

C three

D four

The poet used three stanzas to build the poem. The correct answer is choice C.

The structure of a poem is *most* like ____.

A a song

B a web page

C a story

D a magazine page

A poem is like a song. Songs are made of lines and stanzas, or verses. A web page, story, and magazine page are built of paragraphs. The correct answer is choice A.

What is the main idea of stanza 1?

    A Trees are bare.

    B Apples are red.

    C Winter is dark and cold.

    D Summer is almost over.

    Stanza 1 says goodbye to summer. Days are cooler, and the garden is fading. Some birds have flown away. Summer is almost over. The correct answer is choice D.

What is the main idea of the stanza 2?

    A Robins sing in summer.

    B Autumn is here.

    C Swallows have flown away.

    D Snow falls in winter.

    Stanza 2 tells us that the autumn, or fall, season is here. Leaves are falling, and soon the trees will be bare. Choice B is the correct answer.

What season does stanza 3 tell about?

    A autumn

    B spring

    C summer

    D winter

    It tells about the approaching winter. The bitter winds will whistle and moan, and the days will be cold and dark. Branches will be covered with snow, and the crickets and mice will find warmth inside. Choice D is the correct answer.

How do the stanzas of the poem build on each other? Tell the order of events in this poem.

_____

_____

_____

_____

_____

_____

_____

Did you notice how each stanza is like a paragraph in a story? Each stanza has a main idea. Stanza 1 says good-bye to summer. Stanza 2 tells about autumn. Autumn follows summer. In stanza 3, the speaker talks about winter. Winter comes after autumn. It is the next season of the year. Your answers should tell about the structure of the poem. They should tell about what happens in each stanza. Here is a sample answer:

Stanza 1—The poem begins at the end of summer. The flowers are fading, and the air is cooler. Other birds have flown away, but Robin is still here.

Stanza 2 —The next part of the poem tells that autumn is coming. The leaves are falling, and the apples and pears are ripe. The speaker wonders what Robin will do.

Stanza 3 —This stanza tells that winter is coming. Cold winds will blow, and snow will fall. Mouse and cricket will find warm homes. The speaker worries where Robin will go. The writer builds stanzas of the poem in time order. Each stanza tells about the next season of the year.

UNIT 3 ▓▓
Craft and Structure

How the Robin's Breast Became Red

This is the story of how the robin came to have a red breast, and why the people of the Northland love the robin very much.

Characters:

Hunter

Little Boy

Squirrels, Rabbits, Chipmunks

Indians

Old White Bear

Little Gray Robin

ACT 1, Scene 1

Long ago, in the far Northland, where it was very cold, there was a great blazing fire.

HUNTER *(tossing branches on the fire):* Come, Little Boy, we must work hard to tend this fire. It is the only fire in the whole world.

LITTLE BOY *(carrying twigs):* These twigs will keep the fire burning. We should go back to the woods for more.

Hunter and Little Boy go into the woods. Squirrels, rabbits, and chipmunks creep towards the fire to get warm. Then they hurry away to gather food.

INDIAN #1 *(approaching the fire with a long, flat stick):* We will use these hot coals from the fire to cook our food and keep warm.

INDIAN #2 *(holding a flat stone):* I have brought a stone to carry the coals back to our village.

Indians leave. Hunter and Little Boy return.

HUNTER *(lying down):* Son, I need to rest here on a blanket because I feel ill. You must stay close by and tend the fire. I am counting on you, Little Boy, to keep the fire burning.

Use the library or the Internet to find more information about robins. Where do robins go to get away from cold winter weather?

tend
take care of

LITTLE BOY *(tending the fire):* I have tended the fire for many days and nights. Many times I have left my father to run off into the woods to search for twigs. Then I run back and toss the twigs on the fire. I will not let this fire go out.

ACT 1, Scene 2

WHITE BEAR *(watching from behind a pine tree):* I hate anything warm, but night after night, that fire burns. The hunter's sharp arrows scare me, but Hunter sleeps. Only Little Boy tends the fire.

LITTLE BOY *(rubbing his eyes, yawning):* After many days, father is still not well. I am so very tired. I try to stay awake, but my eyes keep closing… *(head nodding, falling asleep on the ground).*

WHITE BEAR *(laughing to himself, stepping near the fire):* This is my chance! I will put out the only fire in the Northland! *(jumping on the logs with his big, wet feet, tramping the coals)* Go out, fire! I will stamp you and stomp you until no spark remains. *(lumbering back to his cave, laughing)* I have done it! The fire is dead!

ACT 1, Scene 3

LITTLE GRAY ROBIN *(feeling sad):* Oh, no! What has that mean old white bear done? He's put out the only fire in the Northland! *(fluttering down to the fire)* I must take a closer look. *(looking at the ashes)* Oh, no! Wait a minute, I see a tiny spark! One tiny speck of flame. *(hopping about, flapping her wings)* Come on, little spark! Let my wings help you burn brighter. Keep burning, red coal, I can hear you crackle. There is a small flame now. I will fan the flame until it grows brighter and brighter still. *(startled)* Ouch, the flames have scorched me! But, never mind, I am happy that the fire is burning again! *(sitting nearby)* I will stay nearby to keep watch.

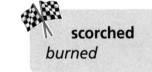
scorched
burned

ACT 1, Scene 4

LITTLE BOY *(awaking to the blazing fire):* I must have been asleep. Is the fire is still burning? It is! Dear Father, wake up, our fire is still burning!

120

Hunter awakes while mean old White Bear stands behind a tree and growls.

LITTLE GRAY ROBIN *(sitting in her tree):* I used to be only a little gray robin, but now my breast has turned a beautiful golden red. It will stay red, and from now on, every robin will have a pretty red breast.

Which *best* describes the setting of the play?

A   in the southern swamps

B   in the far north woods

C   in the western desert

D   in the ocean

The introduction of the play tells us that it takes place in the Northland, where it is very cold. Hunter and Little Boy searched for firewood in the woods. The correct answer is choice B.

What is the *most* important thing the author wants you to know in scene 1 of the play?

A   There was no other fire in the whole world.

B   The Little Gray Robin lived in a hemlock tree.

C   The mean old White Bear hated anything warm.

D   The squirrels, rabbits, and chipmunks warmed their toes by the fire.

The Little Gray Robin lived in a hemlock tree. However, she did not appear in scene 1. Choice B is incorrect. Mean old White Bear does not appear in scene 1, so choice C is not the correct answer. Squirrels, rabbits, and chipmunks warmed their toes by the fire, but that was not the most important idea. Choice D is incorrect. The correct answer is choice A.

What is the problem or conflict in scene 1 of the play?

_____

_____

_____

_____

✓ A problem in a story is the conflict. Conflict is any kind of tension felt. Here is a sample answer:

Hunter and Little Boy tend the fire in scene 1. The fire is the only fire in the Northland. The animals and Indians come to the fire. When Hunter gets sick, Little Boy is in charge of the fire. For days and nights, Little Boy works hard to keep the fire blazing. He knows that he cannot let the fire go out. The reader wonders if Little Boy can keep the fire burning.

How does the conflict build in scene 2?

_____

_____

_____

✓ Think about how the conflict continues. Here is a sample answer:

In scene 2, mean old White Bear watches and waits for Little Boy to fall asleep. White Bear hates anything warm so he hates the fire. He takes his chance to put out the fire. The conflict builds as the fire dies out. White Bear returns to his cave while Hunter and Little Boy sleep.

UNIT 3 ❱❱❱❱❱❱❱❱❱❱❱❱❱❱❱❱❱❱❱❱❱❱❱❱❱❱❱❱❱❱❱❱❱❱❱❱
Craft and Structure

Explain how the conflict is settled in scene 3.

_____

_____

_____

_____

_____

 This asks how the conflict or problem is solved: Here is a sample answer:

Little Gray Robin sees what White Bear did to the fire. She finds a tiny spark in the coal. Then she hops around flapping her wings to fan the small flame. She makes the fire burn brightly once again. The flames scorch her breast and turn it red. Yet, she stays to watch over the fire while Hunter and Little Boy sleep.

Which character in scene 4 tells the reader why all robins have red breasts?

   A   Hunter

   B   Little Boy

   C   White Bear

   D   Little Gray Robin

 In scene 4 Hunter does not speak, so choice A is not the correct answer. White Bear only growls, so choice C is not the correct answer. Little Boy was asleep and did not see what Little Gray Robin did. Choice B is not correct. Little Gray Robin says "…from now on, every robin will have a pretty red breast." The correct answer is choice D.

Test Yourself

bundles
bunches of things tied together

The Squirrel and the Spider

a West African folktale

Chapter 1

After long months of work, a squirrel had made a very fine farm. He had cleared the land, and loosened the soil. He had removed the weeds and planted the seeds. The squirrel reached his fields every day by jumping from tree to tree so he had not bothered to build a road. He smiled as he looked at his fine rows of corn. The corn was ripe and ready to harvest.

A spider went out hunting in the squirrel's neighborhood. During his travels, the spider came to the squirrel's farm and stopped to look at the many rows of corn. The spider searched and searched for a road into the farm, but he found no road.

When the spider returned home, he told his children about the farm. The very next day, they all set out to find it. Right away, they began to build a road to the cornfields. When the road was finished, the clever spider threw pieces of clay pottery along the roadway. He wanted to make believe that his children had dropped them while they worked on the farm.

Chapter 2

The spider and his children began to cut the corn and carry it away. That evening, the squirrel noticed that his fields had been robbed. At first, he could not find the thief, so he decided to keep watch over his cornfields.

Sure enough, the spider soon returned to the fields to steal more of the harvest. The squirrel asked the spider, "What right do you have to these fields of corn?"

The spider replied, "Let me ask you the same question, Squirrel, what right do you have to these fields?"

"They are my fields," answered the squirrel.

"Oh, no!" said the clever spider, "They are mine!"

"But I sowed them and planted them," said the poor squirrel.

"Then where is your road to them?" asked the spider.

"I need no road," answered the squirrel, "I come by the trees."

The spider laughed and continued to use the farm as his own.

Chapter 3

The squirrel could see that the spider was a clever thief. "A squirrel does not need to build a road to a farm," said the squirrel. He hoped that the law would protect him. But the judge decided that no one had ever owned a farm without a road leading to it.

With glee, the spider and his children returned to the farm. They cut down all the corn that was left in the fields. They tied it in huge bundles. Then they went to the market to sell their corn.

When they were almost there, a terrible storm blew in. The spider and his children had to leave their bundles of corn along the road and run for safety. They found a dry place and waited for the storm to end. When the storm passed, the spider and his children returned to pick up their loads of corn.

Chapter 4

When the spider and his children came back to the roadside, they saw a large black crow. Its wide wings were spread out over their bundles of corn to keep them dry.

The spider thanked the crow for taking care of their corn. "Thank you so kindly for taking care of our property," said the spider.

"Your property!" replied the crow. "Who ever heard of anyone leaving their corn by the roadside? These are my bundles of corn."

Surprised, the spider replied, "My children and I harvested this corn. We were carrying it to market, but a storm came up."

"That is nonsense!" shouted the crow, "These bundles of corn are mine!"

The crow picked up all the bundles of corn and flew off. He left the spider and his children with nothing. They returned home in sorrow. The spider had stolen the squirrel's farm, and now he was left with nothing.

sorrow
sadness

1 Explain the structure of Chapter 1. What happened at the beginning, in the middle, and at the end?

_____

_____

_____

_____

2 What happens in Chapter 2 that depended on something in Chapter 1?

_____

_____

_____

_____

3 How did the author build on Chapter 3 to write Chapter 4?

_____

_____

_____

_____

4 Each chapter builds on another to tell a lesson at the very end of the story. Explain the lesson in this folktale, "Those who steal from others often leave empty-handed."

_____

_____

_____

_____

Text Features

RI.3.5

Vocabulary

hyperlink
key words
sidebar

Would you eat a banana without peeling it first? No, of course not! First, it would be hard to eat. Second, it wouldn't taste good. In fact, it would be an awful experience. Text features are like the peel of a banana. You need to get them out of the way first. Read the text features before you read the text. Of course, you can always go back to them if you need help while you read.

Text features get you ready to read. They give you background information that helps you understand the text. Text features give you the clues that make it easier to understand what you are reading. Remember to browse the pages of nonfiction *before you read.*

Key Words

A list of key words is one kind of text feature. Key words give important words and their meanings. Sometimes key words are set in a box. The box may be shaded. It might be found at the top, bottom, or on the sides of a page. Good readers look at the words and their meanings before reading the text. If you get stuck on a word during reading, you can look back at the key words for help.

Read the sample key words box below.

Key Words

root—the underground part of a plant that takes up water
stem—the stalk of a plant
leaf—flat, thin part of green plants that makes food
seed—part of a plant from which new plants grow

Sidebar

A sidebar is another kind of text feature. It is a short box that is printed on the side of text. A sidebar might give new facts. It might make a comment. It may compare something to the text. A sidebar might give an interesting new fact. It might give more information. It might suggest a fun activity.

Read the sample sidebar below.

> **Did you know?**
> Indoor plants fight air pollution. They breathe in carbon dioxide and breathe out clean oxygen.
> Space scientists have been studying plants. They want to find out how to use plants to clean the air in space stations of the future.

Hyperlink

A hyperlink uses the World Wide Web to locate another source of information. By clicking on the highlighted text, the reader can go to a source to find out more about something.

> The leaves of green plants use energy from the sun to make food. This process is known as *photosynthesis.* Visit My Schoolhouse http://www.myschoolhouse.com/courses/O/1/35.asp to find out how photosynthesis works.

Amazing Caves

Caving is a popular adventure sport. People like to explore the underground world. It is very different from above the ground. Some caves have crystals and fossils inside. Other caves may have lakes, streams, or waterfalls. Dripping water leaves minerals behind. These minerals build up. They make strange forms. Formations called stalactites hang down from the ceiling. Other formations called stalagmites stick up from the floor.

Ancient people used caves. They made their homes in caves. Some painted pictures on cave walls. The pictures are still there today. Native Americans, early settlers, pirates, and outlaws have used caves. They needed places to stay warm or cool. Some used them as hideouts.

There are caves all over the world. Some caves are in cold, mountain areas. Some are in hot, tropical rainforests. There are ice caves in Greenland. There are underwater caves in Mexico. There are caves along the coast of Oregon. There are even caves in the deserts of Arizona.

No two caves are alike. The longest cave in the United States is Mammoth Cave in Kentucky. The deepest cave is in Hawaii. The National Park Service website http://www.nature.nps.gov lists parks in the U.S. that offer tours of caves.

Key Words

caver—person who explores caves
caving—exploring caves for fun and adventure
stalactites—icicle-shaped mineral deposits hanging from the ceiling of a cave
stalagmites—cone-shaped mineral deposits built up on a cave floor

Suit Up for Safety!

- Hard hat or helmet with a light
- Waterproof jumpsuit
- Gloves that grip
- Knee pads and elbow pads
- Waterproof boots

Caves are important natural resources. They are living and always growing. They are always changing. Caves are easily damaged. The slightest touch can ruin parts of caves. Animals that live in caves are fragile, too. They should not be disturbed. Cavers need to protect these underground treasures. They need to make sure that caves are there for others to explore.

To learn more about caves and the sport of caving, visit the National Caves Association at http://cavern.com and the National Speleological Society at http://www.caves.org

Save a Cave
- Look but don't touch!
- Respect cave animals.
- Be careful where you step.
- Carry out all trash.

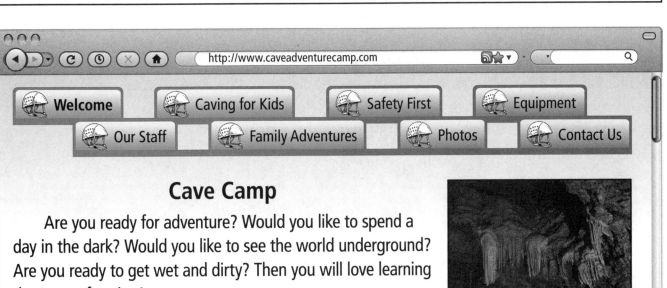

http://www.caveadventurecamp.com

Welcome | Caving for Kids | Safety First | Equipment

Our Staff | Family Adventures | Photos | Contact Us

Cave Camp

Are you ready for adventure? Would you like to spend a day in the dark? Would you like to see the world underground? Are you ready to get wet and dirty? Then you will love learning the sport of caving!

At Cave Adventure Camp, you will climb down into huge dark rooms. You will explore strange rock formations. You will see underground streams and waterfalls. You will walk slippery paths of mud and rocks. You will watch for bats and cave rats!

We put safety first at Cave Adventure Camp. Our campers are fitted with safety gear. It is approved by the National Speleological Society. Campers learn to keep themselves and other campers safe. They learn to protect the cave. Our motto is "Cave safely and cave softly."

Every Cave Adventure Camper is trained in climbing skills. Learn how to keep your footing on uneven ground. Learn to avoid the dangers of deep pits and falling rocks. Learn to crawl through tight and low places. Learn to climb steep spaces. Practice climbing and crawling skills.

Cave Adventure Camp offers safe and fun caving experiences for young people from ages 9–18 and their families. Trained guides will plan cave adventures that meet your skill level. First-timers or experienced cavers, Cave Adventure Camp is right for you.

Pack your flashlight and your camera. Gather your family and friends. Bring a sense of adventure. You will love the sport of caving at Cave Adventure Camp.

Sign up now!

In "Amazing Caves," which text feature highlights important words and their meanings?

A the headings

B a hyperlink

C key words

D a sidebar

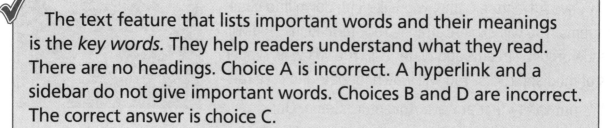

The text feature that lists important words and their meanings is the *key words.* They help readers understand what they read. There are no headings. Choice A is incorrect. A hyperlink and a sidebar do not give important words. Choices B and D are incorrect. The correct answer is choice C.

What is the purpose of the sidebar in "Amazing Caves"?

_____

_____

_____

Think about what information the sidebar gives the reader. Here is a sample answer:

> The sidebar lists the correct clothing for cavers. This clothing is worn to protect cavers. It makes climbing easier. The sidebar gives more facts.

In "Amazing Caves," which text feature connects the reader to a website with more information about caving?

A the sidebar

B the key words

C the hyperlink

D the art

The hyperlink sends the reader to a website. There the reader can learn more about caving. The sidebar gives more facts. It does not send the reader to a website. The key words are important words and their meanings. This list does not send the reader to a website. The art does not connect to a website. Choices A, B, and D are incorrect. The correct answer is choice C.

Which term *best* describes the structure of "Cave Camp"?

A a story

B a letter

C a website

D a textbook page

"Cave Camp" is the web page for Cave Adventure Camp. The welcome page tells about the camp. A user can click on buttons to find more information. The passage is not written in the form of a letter. Choice B is incorrect. It is not a story with characters and a setting. Choice A is incorrect. It is not written in the form of a textbook page. Choice D is incorrect. The correct answer is choice C.

In "Cave Camp," what text feature shows that the camp follows national standards for safety?

_____

_____

_____

_____

Think about the purpose of each text feature. Here is a sample answer:

The website says that the camp uses the right safety gear. It has a hyperlink to the National Speleological Society. Readers can click on the hyperlink. When they open it, they can find the national standards.

Test Yourself

Read the two passages. Then answer the questions.

Happy Birthday, SUE!

You are invited to SUE's 10th birthday party. SUE is at home in Chicago. So far, more than sixteen million people have visited SUE. Are *you* ready to party? All of us at the Field Museum are excited. We hope to see you here.

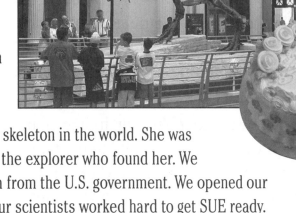

SUE is the largest *T. rex* skeleton in the world. She was named for Sue Hendrickson, the explorer who found her. We purchased the *T. rex* skeleton from the U.S. government. We opened our SUE exhibit ten years ago. Our scientists worked hard to get SUE ready. Now we are getting her ready for her big party.

Would you like to find out more about SUE? Visit our website: http://www.fieldmuseum.org/sue/#index. Watch a short video of the new 3-D movie, "Waking the *T. rex*: the Story of SUE." Sign up for a night at the museum. Bring a friend to Dozin' with the Dinos, a birthday sleepover. Learn more about SUE's bones. Read about her trip from the fields of South Dakota to the Field Museum. Meet our scientists who study dinosaurs. Ask one of our dinosaur experts a question. Look at SUE's photos and videos. Find museum directions and hours. You can order tickets online. Visit our museum store. And don't forget to send a birthday note to SUE.

Meet Sue Hendrickson, Explorer

It happened one day in August, 1990. That was the day that Sue Hendrickson became famous. Sue had joined a team of explorers on a dinosaur dig. They were hunting for fossils in the Black Hills of South Dakota. She found a reddish-brown rock. Then she found a string of small bones. These bones led her to huge dinosaur backbones. They led to an almost complete dinosaur skeleton.

Sue Hendrickson found the largest *Tyrannosaurus rex* skeleton ever. It was also the most complete set of *T. rex* bones. They were in very good condition. The dinosaur skeleton was named SUE after Sue Hendrickson. Now everyone knew her name. She was famous.

Sue Hendrickson was born in Chicago, Illinois. She grew up near Munster, Indiana. Sue Hendrickson was the middle child in her family. She was a shy little girl who enjoyed reading. Even as a young girl, Sue loved to look for and find things. She joined the swim team when she was a teen. She loved swimming and spending time in the water. Sue became a woman who loved adventure. She became a diver and explored the sea floor. She collected insect fossils. Sue taught herself to become a fossil hunter.

After finding the *T. rex*, Sue Hendrickson joined a team of underwater explorers. She has joined the marine archaeologists on many dives. They explore shipwrecks, sunken treasure, and very old, sunken cities.

Key Words

Tyrannosaurus rex—the largest of the huge, two-footed, flesh-eating dinosaurs
fossil—any hardened remains of a plant or animal of a previous geological period, preserved in the earth's crust
skeleton—the hard framework of the bones of an animal
marine archaeologist—a person who studies the life of ancient peoples by uncovering ancient cities or items under the sea
passion—strong emotion or desire

Sue Hendrickson loves her work. She says it is her passion. She feels lucky that her work lets her do what she loves to do. Sue Hendrickson enjoys the excitement of searching for things. She thinks that it is worth the hard work. The thrill of finding things keeps her going. Sue says that she feels like a child who never grew up.

The Field Museum in Chicago bought the *T. rex* skeleton. *T. rex* SUE is on display for thousands to see. Sue hopes that more children grow up to be explorers. She knows that learning about the past is important. There are many more things to discover in our world.

For more information, visit www.suehendrickson.com.

I wonder...
How old was SUE when she died?
Like counting tree rings, scientists counted the rings in SUE's bones. They have found that SUE was 28 years old when she died. Scientists believe that the *T. rex* did not live more than 30 years. In fact, SUE is the oldest *T. rex* discovered so far.

1 Which of these *best* describes the overall structure of "Happy Birthday, SUE"?

A a story

B a diary

C an advertisement

D a textbook page

2 In "Happy Birthday, SUE," what text feature could you add to help you easily find information?

A hyperlink

B sidebar

C photographs

D key words

3 Which of the following choices *best* describes the structure of "Meet Sue Hendrickson, Explorer"?

    A a play

    B a letter

    C a website page

    D a magazine article

4 Why is it important for the reader to look at and read text features before reading the text on a page?

_____

_____

_____

_____

_____

5 What feature of text would be *most* helpful to read *before* reading "Meet Sue Hendrickson, Explorer"?

    A art

    B sidebar

    C key words

    D hyperlink

6 Which text feature in "Meet Sue Hendrickson, Explorer" tells what scientists did to figure out how old SUE was when she died?

    A art

    B sidebar

    C hyperlink

    D key words

Point of View and Author's Purpose

RL.3.6, RI.3.6

Vocabulary

convince

equal rights

government

justice

lyrics

women's
  suffrage

All writing has a **point of view.** In fiction, stories can be told from a character's point of view. They could also be told from a narrator's point of view. A poem is told from the point of view of a speaker.

Nonfiction has a point of view, too. Imagine that you are reading a story about camping. From the point of view of the narrator, outdoor camping is fun and exciting. It is a way to stay close to nature. Someone whose camping trip was rainy and buggy would write from a different point of view. Each story would be told in a different way. The mood of each story would be different.

When you read, it is important to think about who is telling the story. Think about how the story is being told. Think about why it is being told. Think about the **author's purpose** for writing.

Point of View in Literary Text

When you read, you must ask, *Who is telling this story?* In some stories, a character tells the story. This is called the **first-person point of view.** The character uses the pronouns *I* and *we.*

Other stories are told from the **third-person point of view.** A narrator tells the story. The narrator uses the pronouns *he, she,* or *they.* The narrator may write from the point of view of one or more characters. Sometimes the narrator writes from the point of view of someone outside the story.

Just Ask a Student

Dear Editor,

Ask most students, and they will tell you that their favorite subject is recess. Not me! I am a third grader, and I hate recess. Many students complain that our school has cut our recess time. Our principal says that teachers need more time to teach. But less recess time is fine with me.

The main reason I do not like recess is that we do not play. Too many students just want to hang out and do nothing. If we do decide to start a game, it takes forever to get a team together. By the time we work out the team and the rules, there is no time left to play. When we do play, it usually ends in a fight. The rules get so complicated that nobody can follow them. The game falls apart, arguments start, and fights break out. Someone gets hurt. Then the playground aide sends one person to the nurse and another person to the principal's office. The rest of us go back to class feeling sweaty, frustrated, and mad. It happens all the time.

They should just ask a student! I would tell them that recess would be a lot more fun if an adult, like a coach, could help us on the playground at recess. We do not need someone who just watches us. We need an adult who will participate and play with us. There would be a lot more physical activity if a coach could help us organize teams and set the rules. More students would play if a coach could help us keep a game going. It would help us avoid a lot of fights. I know that I would feel a lot safer. We would all have a lot more fun. More students would get exercise. I wish that someone would listen to what I think. It would help us students go back to class feeling better and ready to learn.

Amir

What is the point of view of this story?

A first person

B third person, told by a narrator outside the story

C third person, from the point of view of one character

D third person, revealing the thoughts of several characters

 This is a letter written by a student. A letter is written in first person. If you did not know this, a clue would be the pronoun *I*. This tells us that it is first person. The correct answer is choice A.

How does Amir's point of view differ from the point of view of other students?

_____

_____

 Think about what Amir writes. Then think about what other students might think. Here is a sample answer:

> Most students like recess. The narrator does not. To him, recess is a terrible idea. He would like some changes made to recess.

Describe what Amir wants adults to do during recess.

_____

_____

 Amir wants adults to help. Here is a sample answer:

> Amir wants adults to structure recess more. He wants them to organize games for the students.

Do you share Amir's point of view on recess? Why or why not?

_____

_____

_____

_____

You may agree with Amir because you have felt the same feelings. Or, you may disagree that you do not want more structure in recess. Either way, you bring your own experience. This means that you have a point of view that is your very own. Here is a sample answer:

> I love recess and do not agree with Amir. Recess is the one time of the day when we can move around and do not have to sit still. I would not like recess to be structured like classtime. At recess, my friends and I can do what we want to do. Adults are not telling us what to do.

Read the story. Then answer the questions.

The Great Field Trip Debate

Mr. Ruiz is the coolest science teacher ever! He brings all kinds of stuff to share with his class—bugs, rocks, plants, even a meteorite. He lets his students look at them up close. His class got to hold a heavy hunk of rock from outer space.

Mr. Ruiz likes his students to ask questions. He even asks their help in making decisions. This week, they talked about the class field trip. From a list of five places, the class narrowed it down to two choices: a visit to the planetarium or a trip to the nature center. Mr. Robinson had his students choose one place. Then he split them into two groups based on the place they

UNIT 3 ▨▨▨▨▨▨▨▨▨▨▨▨▨▨▨▨▨▨▨▨▨▨▨▨▨▨▨▨▨▨▨
Craft and Structure

picked. Each group will get 5 minutes to convince the rest of the class to agree with their choice. Then they will vote on which place to visit.

Here are the first group's reasons to pick the nature center. Kayla's group likes to spend time outdoors. They do not like to sit inside all day. The nature center has tour guides and live animal exhibits. Kayla's group says they like checking out the animal skulls, furs, tracks, and feathers on display. They can search for native plants and see how they grow. Kayla's group wants to learn how to make solar-powered ovens. Then they can use them to cook hot dogs and chocolate marshmallow treats for lunch. In the afternoon, they can go on a treasure hunt along the hiking trails. Kayla's group likes using maps and compasses to find their way around.

Kayla's friend Julio is in the other group. Julio's group likes the idea of going into the city to the planetarium. They say that many students have never been to a planetarium. Even though it is a long bus ride, it could be their best chance to go. They went online and found out that the planetarium has a new show. It is about the new planets astronomers have discovered. These planets could support life. Julio loves to imagine what real space aliens look like! His group says that the planetarium has an enormous lunchroom. They want the class to pack their lunches and buy drinks and snacks. They say that the planetarium's gift shop is amazing!

Well, the voting is over. Guess what? It is a tie! What will Mr. Robinson do now?

What is the point of view of this story?

A first person

B third person, told by a speaker outside the story

C third person, from the point of view of one character

D third person, revealing the thoughts of several characters

There is no *I* in this story. That rules out choice A. The narrator uses the pronouns *he, she,* and *they.* This story is told from the **third-person** point of view. The narrator does not express the point of view of only one character. Choice C is incorrect. The narrator does not tell the thoughts of more than one character. Choice D is incorrect. The narrator expresses the point of view of someone outside the story. The correct answer is choice B.

With which group's point of view would you agree?
Explain your choice.

_____

_____

_____

_____

_____

You have read the story. Know that your point of view is just as good as anyone else's. Here is a sample answer:

I have never been to a planetarium. I read that astronomers have discovered new planets. They think that these planets might support life. I would like to learn more about them. I have been to the nature center before. It would be worth the long bus ride into the city to go to the planetarium.

Describe how the passages are different in terms of point of view.

_____

_____

_____

_____

_____

_____

_____

_____

_____

✔ **Think about who is telling the story or giving an opinion. Here is a sample answer:**

The first passage is a **first-person** point of view. It tells one boy's feelings about recess. He knows that students need more exercise. But he says recess is not doing that. He wishes that grown-ups would ask him. He would tell them how to make recess safer and more fun. He gives ideas to help students join in at recess.

The second story is a **third-person** point of view. The narrator is someone outside the story. The narrator tells how a teacher helps his class choose a field trip. The class picks two field trip ideas. The narrator tells the reasons for both choices. But the narrator does not say which one is better.

Point of View in Informational Text

A piece of writing about ideas or facts also has a point of view. The point of view is the author's. The point of view may depend on the **author's purpose** for writing. When two people have very different reasons for writing, their writings show different points of view.

Think of a playground accident. A playground aide comes to the scene. She writes a report about what she saw. The playground aide does not take sides. She needs to **inform** or **explain** what happened to the principal.

Now think about a playground accident from the point of view of the student who was hurt. He may believe he did nothing wrong. He was the victim. He believes that it was the other student who caused the accident. He will try to **persuade** the principal that it was not his fault.

Now imagine that you have just witnessed the accident. You write an email to your friend about the accident you saw. Chances are you are writing to **describe** what happened.

Guided Practice

Read the passage. Then answer the questions.

Suffrage Songs

Music has always helped people share their feelings. The words tell the songwriter's point of view. The words of songs can also change a listener's point of view. Songs about women's voting rights did just that.

In the early 1900s, there were hundreds of songs about women's right to vote. Songwriters wrote new lyrics for popular tunes. They wrote words that asked important questions. Sometimes, they laughed at the old ways. The lyrics poked fun at people who would not change. Songwriters shared their own point of views. Artists drew pictures for the covers of music. They often showed strong and powerful American women.

> **women's suffrage**
> *the battle for voting rights for women*

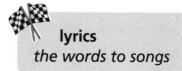

> **lyrics**
> *the words to songs*

Women's suffrage songs spoke to every American, women and men. Tunes were catchy and easy to remember. Rhymes made them easy to sing. Women could see themselves in the words of the songs. Some songs told about the things women have done for their country. Others told about the good things they do every day. Some told about what women could do in America's future. A song might make some women pay more attention. It might make them think, read, or talk about voting rights. It might make some women want to join the movement. It might make others want to vote. A man listening to a suffrage song might see himself in some of the words. It might show him that men owe much to women. It might show him that it would not be so bad to allow women to vote.

This was a time when people were surrounded by ads, newspapers, and magazines. All told their point of views. Songs were a great way to spread thoughts and ideas. Songs also changed feelings or moods. Men and women could find something in a song that was true about their lives. Songs got people fired up. Music became a good way to convince Americans that women should have the right to vote.

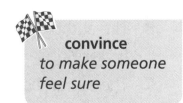

convince
to make someone feel sure

What is the point of view of "Suffrage Songs"?

   A   first person

   B   third person, told by a narrator

   C   third person, from the point of view of one character

   D   third person, revealing the thoughts of several characters

   The pronouns *I* and *we* are not used in this passage. The passage is not written from the first-person point of view. Choice A is incorrect. The passage does not have characters in it. Choices C and D are incorrect. An outside narrator explains about suffrage songs. Choice B is the correct answer.

Which statement *best* describes the author's point of view?

   A   The author thinks that suffrage songs destroyed America.

   B   The author believes that suffrage songs made women feel silly.

   C   The author believes that suffrage songs did not make people think about women's right to vote.

   D   The author feels that suffrage songs were important in the fight for women's right to vote.

   The author says that suffrage songs were important. The author did not say that the songs destroyed America. Choice A is incorrect. The author did not say that suffrage songs made women feel silly. Choice B is incorrect. The author did not say that the songs did not make people think about women's right to vote. Choice C is incorrect. The correct answer is choice D.

UNIT 3 ✖✖✖✖✖✖✖✖✖✖✖✖✖✖✖✖✖✖✖✖✖✖✖✖✖✖✖✖✖✖✖✖✖✖✖✖✖✖✖
Craft and Structure

What was the author's purpose for writing "Suffrage Songs"?

_____

_____

_____

_____

_____

_____

 Think about why the author wrote this passage. Was it to entertain the reader? Maybe, he wanted to persuade the reader. Here is a sample answer:

The purpose of "Suffrage Songs" was to explain how songs played an important part in the fight for women's rights. It tells how songs drew attention to the cause. Songs were easy to sing and remember. Songs spoke to both women and men. They made people think, read, and talk about equal rights. They made women want to vote. They helped men know that it would not be a bad idea.

Test Yourself

Passage 1

The Constitution is the supreme law of the United States.

Justice for All

by Susan B. Anthony

In 1783, the U.S. Constitution gave white men who owned property the right to vote. Eighty years later, nonwhite men were given that right. Now, it is 1870. Women still do not have the right to vote in America. How much longer must we wait? Women of America, wake up!

I believe in equal rights for all Americans. My friend Elizabeth Cady Stanton and I believe that a woman's right to vote is a good first step. Women should be able to vote for things that women care about. This will lead to better lives for everyone.

Many women do not agree. Some say they do not want to vote. They want the law to stay the same. Women are too busy. They take care of their homes and families. Some are only interested in their own communities. They say that thinking about our laws is not what women were born to do.

Most men think that our ideas are silly. Many say that it is their job to protect women. Voting is not for ladies. Some say that women are not smart enough to vote. It is not in their nature. They believe that women should just take care of their families and homes. Some say that if women get the right to vote, it will destroy our country. Others say that women do not deserve to vote. They do not fight to defend their country.

equal rights
the same powers and privileges for everyone under the law

For 30 years, I have spoken out about women's rights. I travel all over the country. I organize rallies. We wave flags, sing songs, and read poems. We spread the word with our newspaper. I believe that women can do more than men think we can. Women are strong and smart. They should not depend on men to protect them. It is true that women do not go to war. But they send their sons to war.

I gathered letters with thousands of signatures from 26 states. When I took these letters to Congress, they just laughed. For many years, I talked to every Congress about equal rights for women. For days, I stood with other women outside the White House. We tried to get President Wilson's attention. Some people made fun of us and called us names. They still write bad things about us in the newspapers. But we will not give up! It's time to demand justice for all Americans!

Susan B. Anthony did not live to see the law changed. She died in 1906 before all adult women in the United States received the right to vote. Congress passed the Nineteenth Amendment to the U.S. Constitution in 1920. The battle for a woman's right to vote had taken more than 220 years!

Congress is the elected members of government who represent the people.

justice
fairness

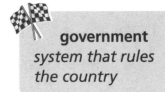

government
system that rules the country

Passage 2

Oh Dear, What Can the Matter Be?

by L. May Wheeler

This song was sung to the tune of a nursery rhyme of the 1880s. It became popular again during the fight for American women's right to vote. The song was sung at rallies and meetings.

Chorus:

Oh dear, what can the matter be?
Dear, dear what can the matter be?
Oh dear, what can the matter be?
Women are wanting to vote.

Verses:

Women have husbands; they are protected.
Women have sons by whom they're directed.
Women have fathers; they're not neglected.
Why are they wanting to vote?

Women have homes where they should labor.
Women have children whom they should favor.
Women have time to visit each neighbor.
Why are they wanting to vote?

Women have raised all the sons of the brave.
Women have shared in the service they gave
Women have worked for this country to save.
And that's why we're going to vote!

Final Chorus:

Oh, dear, what can the matter be?
Dear, dear what can the matter be?
Oh dear, what can the matter be?
Why should men get every vote?

1   What is the author's point of view in passage 1?

   A   first person

   B   third person, told by a narrator outside the story

   C   third person, from the point of view of one character

   D   third person, revealing the thoughts of several characters

2   In passage 2, how does point of view influence the story?
    How might the story be different if a man were the
    narrator?

    _____

    _____

    _____

    _____

    _____

3 Which of these statements would *best* agree with Susan B. Anthony's point of view in passage 1?

   A Women already have everything they need.

   B Women deserve better than their grandmothers had.

   C If women get the right to vote, it will destroy our country.

   D If women want to vote, then they should join the military.

4 What is the author's purpose in passage 1?

   A to inform

   B to persuade

   C to describe

   D to entertain

5 Explain the author's purpose in writing passage 2.

_____

_____

_____

_____

_____

REVIEW

Craft and Structure

Vocabulary
daylight
saving time

schedule

standard time

time zones

Read the passage. Then answer the questions.

How Maui Captured the Sun
A Hawaiian Legend

Characters:

Narrator

Maui

Kuakino, the Elder

Kuakino People Group #1 (6 people)

Kuakino People Group #2 (3 people)

The Sun

The Kupe'e *(shellfish)*

Act 1, Scene 1

The scene is set on the shores of the island of Maui in the Hawaiian Islands.

NARRATOR: Long ago, the sun traveled across the Hawaiian sky. Sometimes it went fast. Sometimes it went slow. The people could not count on it.

KUAKINO, THE ELDER *(angrily):* Sometimes the sun will not rise. Night lasts for a very long time. The land is dark and cold. Our plants cannot grow. Fishing is difficult.

KUAKINO GROUP #1: Sometimes, the sun just stays out. The heat is terrible. Trees and plants are burned. Ponds are dried up. Everyone is overheated.

KUAKINO GROUP #2: The ground is cracked. The rocks are too hot to touch. We can do nothing to change the sun's travels.

KUAKINO GROUP #1: When the sun rises, it speeds across the sky. Some days the sun travels very slowly. It travels close to the ground and burns the land.

KUAKINO, THE ELDER: The sun teases us and laughs at us.

Scene 2

The scene is set along a road near fields where the Kuakino people are farming.

NARRATOR: One day, Maui traveled to Koloa. When he rested, he watched the Kuakino family work.

MAUI *(walking to the canoe shed):* I am traveling on a long trip. I am hungry. Does your family have any food to share?

KUAKINO, THE ELDER: My people have not eaten today. But you are welcome to our food.

MAUI *(eating):* Your people have given me their sweetest fish and potatoes. I am grateful. I am going to do something important. The sun is making you all suffer. I am going to go to the mountain and slow down the sun.

KUAKINO, THE ELDER and HIS PEOPLE *(amazed):* Who are you? That is a very risky plan. How can you slow down the sun?

MAUI *(showing his tattoo):* I am Maui. I am the grandson of Hina, warrior of the gods. I am going to the mountain. I will take my magical jawbone, my stone club, and a trap. My magic songs will weaken the sun.

Act 2, Scene 1

The scene is set at the bottom of the mountain.

KUAKINO, THE ELDER: Maui is hidden in the sand. We know that the sun likes to make mischief when he is awake. We need to fill the sun's stomach so he will sleep for a long time. Then Maui can climb the mountain.

THE KUPE'E: We will help Maui. We will give ourselves up to be cooked. Then you can leave us as food for the sun to see and smell.

NARRATOR: The plan worked. The sun rose and smelled the cooked Kupe'e. The sun was so full it moved slowly across the sky. Then, it sank into the sea. The sun snored all night. Maui's body was changed back to a human. He climbed the mountain, sang songs to the sun, and made the sun weak.

Scene 2

The scene is set on top of the mountain.

MAUI: Sun, you must follow the rules. From this day on, you must let the people and animals live. Let the plants grow.

NARRATOR: The sun agreed. Maui set it loose. The sun slowly traveled across the sky. Then it sank in the west. All was well.

1 This play is structured as _____ .

   A chapters

   B paragraphs

   C acts and scenes

   D lines and stanzas

2 Which of these is a setting in the play?

   A at a lake

   B in a village

   C near a swamp

   D at the top of a mountain

3 Whose point of view is *not* presented in this play?

   A Maui's

   B The Sun's

   C The Kupe'e's

   D Kuakino, the Elder's

UNIT 3 ✖✖✖✖✖✖✖✖✖✖✖✖✖✖✖✖✖✖✖✖✖✖✖✖✖✖✖✖✖✖✖✖✖✖✖✖✖✖✖
Craft and Structure

4 In Act 1, Scene 2, how would you contrast the feelings of the Kuakino people with Maui's about his plan to slow the sun?

_____

_____

_____

_____

5 What happens in Act 2, Scene 1 that makes the reader read on to find out what happens?

A The reader wonders if Maui will fail.

B The reader wonders if Maui will succeed.

C The reader wonders if the Kupe'e will help Maui.

D all of the above

Read the poem. Then answer the questions.

Bed in Summer

by Robert Louis Stevenson

1 In winter I get up at night
2 And dress by yellow candle-light.
3 In summer, quite the other way,
4 I have to go to bed by day.

5 I have to go to bed and see
6 The birds still hopping on the tree,
7 Or hear the grown-up people's feet
8 Still going past me in the street.

9 And does it not seem hard to you,
10 When all the sky is clear and blue,
11 And I should like so much to play,
12 To have to go to bed by day?

6 Which structure does this poem use?

   A acts

   B stanzas

   C chapters

   D paragraphs

7 This passage is written from which point of view?

   A first person, a child

   B third person, one character

   C third person, outside narrator

   D third person, more than one character

8 Briefly tell the main idea of this passage. Then explain why you agree or disagree with the point of view of the speaker.

   _____

   _____

   _____

   _____

9 Which part of the passage contrasts summer and winter?

   A the title

   B the first stanza

   C the second stanza

   D the third stanza

Passage 1

Spring Forward and Fall Back

In spring, most Americans set their clocks ahead by one hour. They set their clocks back by one hour in fall. That is why they use the saying "spring forward and fall back." It helps them to remember what time to set their clocks. People in Hawaii and most of Arizona do not change their clocks. They keep standard time all year long.

Daylight saving time begins the second Sunday in March. This means we get an extra hour of sunlight each evening. That is when most people are awake and busy. Daylight saving time lets children play outdoors longer. It lets people enjoy parks and playgrounds longer. People can do more shopping or working outdoors. There are fewer traffic accidents. There is much less crime. Daylight saving time also saves energy.

Daylight saving time may not be good for farmers and others who get up early. It stays darker in the early morning hours. They may have to start work in the dark. Daylight saving time ends the first Sunday in November.

Standard Time   Daylight Saving Time

Back in the early days of our country, local governments set their own time. The country was a patchwork of time. It was very confusing. Benjamin Franklin first came up with an idea to save daylight hours. Then the first railroads were built across America. People needed train schedules they could depend on. The railroads set time zones all across the country. They set the time in each time zone. It became law. Many changes were made to daylight saving time. There is still no law that says towns, counties, or states must change to daylight saving time. In most of the country, people enjoy the extra hours of daylight. Visit http://www.webexhibits.org/daylightsaving/b.html to learn more.

Key Words

standard time—the official time of a country or region
daylight saving time—time that is one hour later than standard time
schedule—a timetable or plan for a certain time
time zones—areas around the world, in which the same standard is used; there are 24 time zones

Do We Have to Fall Back?

Dear Editor,

I am writing to ask a very simple question: Why do we have to turn our clocks back one hour in the fall? I can see that the days are getting shorter already. It is hard to get used to it getting dark this early.

I used to stay out and play until 9 o'clock. Then it was 8 o'clock. Tonight, it was not even 7 o'clock, and the streetlights came on. (That is Mom's signal to come inside.) Now, I just found out that in a couple of weeks, our clocks go back one hour. Good-bye daylight savings time! That means it will be dark before 6 o'clock, then before 5 o'clock. I know it will only get worse.

It is bad enough that I have homework to do before I can go out to play after school. When daylight saving time ends, there will be no daylight left, no chance to go outside and play. Kids need fresh air and exercise! That means the end of football practice. I will be coming home from karate class in the dark. I will be coming home from scout meetings in the dark. I'll be taking out the trash in the dark. I will be shoveling snow in the dark. The only thing that I'll be doing in the daylight is going to school. That is just not right!

Whose idea was it to turn the clocks back in the late fall? It does not make sense. Winter is dark enough! Why go back to standard time at all? I think that we should keep daylight saving time all year.

Jamal

10 Which text feature explains important terms used in passage 1?

A sidebar

B hyperlinks

C illustration

D key words

11 Passage 2 is a ____.

    A web page

    B textbook page

    C a letter to give opinion

    D a map to provide directions

12 The author of passage 1 ____.

    A expresses his opinion of daylight saving time

    B informs the reader about daylight saving time

    C asks questions about daylight saving time

    D blames daylight saving time on the government

13 Both authors would agree that ____.

    A people enjoy extra hours of daylight

    B daylight saving time is a dumb idea

    C daylight saving time saves energy

    D children should trick-or-treat in the daylight

14 The content and style of passage 1 would *not* be found ____.

    A in a magazine

    B on a company's web page

    C on the page of a textbook

    D in a someone's personal diary

15 Compare the authors' point of views in the two passages.
Fill in the graphic organizer to answer the questions about
the author's point of view of each passage.

Spring Forward, Fall Back		Do We Have to Fall Back?
	Why did the author write this passage? (author's purpose)	
	Whom is the author writing to?	
	What is the point of view of the passage?	

Integration of Knowledge and Ideas

UNIT 4

Good readers make connections. They look at pictures, maps, and graphs. They then connect these to what they are reading. They compare and contrast stories, characters, and themes. This helps to better understand stories.

Reading more than one factual text about the same subject can help, too. When you read from two sources, you are better able to understand the things you read. It can tell you whether or not what you are reading is true. This way you can better know what is fact and what is opinion.

This unit is all about how you take in ideas from your reading. It is about what you learn from the different things you read. And it is about how you use that information.

- **In Lesson 11,** you will learn how pictures help you understand text. You will also learn how reading more than one text on the same topic can help you answer questions.

- **Lesson 12** is about what you read in your texts. You'll learn how to tell if you are really reading facts. You will also learn things like cause and effect, as well as sequence.

- **In Lesson 13,** you will learn to look at texts side by side. You will see things that are similar. You will see things that are different. These things will help you understand your text.

Visual Literacy

RL.3.7, RI.3.7

Have you ever asked why books have pictures? Have you seen pictures in newspapers? Pictures, maps, and charts can help you learn from what you read. They can give you extra information. Sometimes, you get more information from a picture than you do from words!

Guided Practice

Read the passage. Then answer the questions.

allowance
sum of money given each week or month

The Messy Room

by Catherine Bevard

"That room better be clean by dinner time!" Tommy's mom yelled up the stairs. Tommy looked around his room. It was a mess! He had never been good at keeping his room clean. But this time it was really bad. There were candy wrappers on the floor and books under the bed. There were empty juice boxes on the dresser and movies on the chair. Every day when Tommy got home from school, he threw his clothes on the floor. These were just a few things that made Tommy's room messy. There was stuff everywhere!

Tommy had tried to get out of cleaning his room. First, he had said he was sick. He had pretended to cough and sneeze, for hours on end, but that did not work for very long. Somehow, his parents knew he was faking! Then Tommy had tried to hide everything under his bed. But, there was too much mess to hide under there. Finally, Tommy had tried to push everything into his closet, but by the time everything was put in, the door would not close. Tommy realized he would have to do it. He would have to clean up his room.

Hours went by, and Tommy sorted, cleaned, threw away garbage, and put away toys and books. The whole time, he was complaining. "Why should I have to clean my room?" he said. "I do not want to do this!"

"Look here," he said. Sticking out from under his bed was a small, white envelope. "What is that?" he said. He went closer. When he finally pulled the envelope out, he opened it up. Inside, there was allowance money that he had been saving! Tommy's room had been so messy that he had lost the money and forgotten about it. Now, Tommy not only had a clean room, but he had his allowance money, too!

As Tommy skipped down the stairs for dinner, he turned to his mom. "You are right!" he said. "Cleaning my room is great! I should do it more often!"

Which detail of the story is *best* shown by the illustration?

A Tommy's dresser had empty juice boxes on it.

B Tommy's mother wanted him to clean his room.

C The mess in Tommy's room was out of control.

D Tommy found allowance money in his room.

Look at the illustration. It shows Tommy in his room. However, it does not show his dresser. Also, it does not show Tommy's mom or his allowance money. This just shows the entire mess. Choice C is the correct answer.

The illustration can help you understand _____.

  A how Tommy's room got so messy

  B when Tommy lost his allowance money

  C why Tommy does not want to clean his room

  D why Tommy's mom seems angry in the story

You can get rid of some choices right away. The illustration does not tell *how* anything happened. It just shows the way something is. Also, the illustration does not tell us *when* something happened. It does not tell why Tommy does not want to clean his room. We do not know if he likes it messy or if he just does not have time to clean it. The illustration does show how messy the room is. This could be a reason that Tommy's mom seems angry. Choice D is the correct answer.

How does the illustration add to your understanding of the story?

_____

_____

_____

Here is a sample answer:

The illustration helps us understand the setting.
The words in the story explain the mess in Tommy's room.
The illustration helps us see how bad it really is!

hollow
empty

Washington Monument

by Catherine Bevard

Have you seen the Washington Monument? You may have seen a picture of it. It was expensive to build. People started raising money to build it in the 1830s. When money ran out, there was a very long delay in its construction. The monument was not finished until 1884! In 1888, it opened to the public.

The monument was built to honor George Washington. The money for it came from donations. At first, people could only donate a dollar to the cause. After the long delay in building, President Grant signed a bill for the money to finish it.

This large wonder is in Washington, D.C. This is our nation's capital. The monument is 555 feet tall. What a climb! To get to the top, you have to climb 897 stairs. It is made of marble. In strong winds of over 20 miles per hour, it moves a bit. It does not sway enough to be dangerous. It is hollow inside. It was once the largest structure in the world. That has changed now, but it is still quite a sight to see. It is still the largest stone structure in the world.

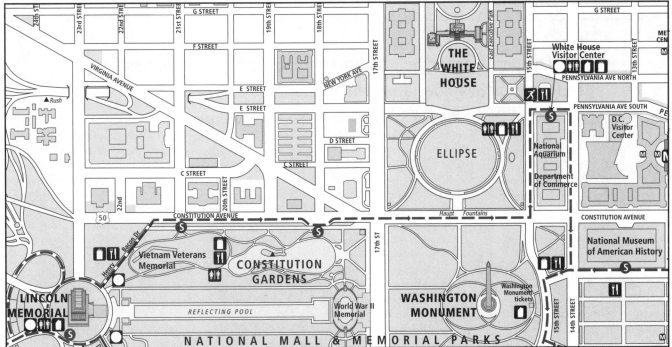

Which detail is shown in the photograph, but is *not* described in the article about the Washington Monument?

    A The Washington Monument is very tall.

    B It took years to finish building the Washington Monument.

    C There is a reflecting pool in front of the monument.

    D People started raising money for the monument in the 1830s.

The photograph shows a reflecting pool. The pool is in front of the monument. The text does not tell what is around the monument. Choice C is the correct answer.

Name one thing that the photograph helps you understand about the Washington Monument.

_____

_____

_____

Here is a sample response:

    The photograph helps show the size of the monument. The article tells how large the monument is. The picture shows us what it looks like and gives us a visual aid.

What does the map help you understand about the text?

_____

_____

_____

✓ **The map gives details that the photograph and the text do not. Here is a sample answer:**

The article does not tell you how close the monument is to the White House. The map shows what is around the monument. This is information you cannot get from the text.

Imagine that your teacher asked you to write a report about the Washington Monument. Using the article, the map, and the photograph, list four things you could include in the report.

1. _____

2. _____

3. _____

4. _____

✓ **If you were writing a report on the Washington Monument, you could tell what it looks like. You could tell what is near it and you could give details about it. Here is a sample answer:**

1. The monument is near the White House.
2. It is 555 feet tall.
3. There is water in front of it.
4. It opened to the public in 1888.

Test Yourself

Mount Rushmore

Have you ever seen a face in a mountain? It sounds crazy. That is what Mount Rushmore is. The mountain shows the faces of four presidents. The presidents are George Washington, Thomas Jefferson, Abraham Lincoln, and Theodore Roosevelt.

This landmark is in the Black Hills of South Dakota. A man studying South Dakota history came up with this idea in 1923. The carving did not begin until 1927.

The faces were carved by Gutzon Borglum. He used dynamite. This got rid of much of the rock on the mountain. Under the rock, there was only 3–6 inches of granite left. This is where he carved the faces. There were supposed to be more than faces. The carving was supposed to go down to the waist. But there was no money to finish it.

The carver had help. He had 400 men help him work on the mountain. They worked on it for over ten years. The men made Washington

Native Americans called this mountain "Six Grandfathers."

Men working on Mount Rushmore

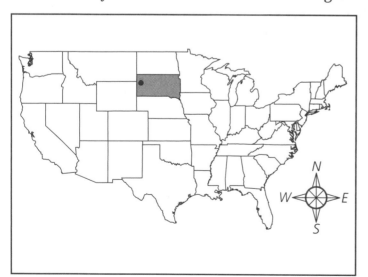

Mount Rushmore in South Dakota. Each head is as tall as a six-story building.

first. Then they started Jefferson. He was supposed to be to the right of Washington. But there were cracks in the rock. The carving had to be destroyed. They started again. This time Jefferson was on Washington's left.

The carving stopped in 1941. Many people visit the site every year. They are amazed. The faces really look like the presidents. Each head is as tall as a six-story building.

1 What does photograph 1 show that the other photographs do not?

_____

_____

_____

_____

_____

2 What can you tell by looking at photograph 2?

   A The faces are very large.

   B Mount Rushmore is in South Dakota.

   C It did not take much time to carve Mount Rushmore.

   D The carvings were supposed to go down to the waist.

3 List four facts about Mount Rushmore using the photographs, the map, and the passage.

   1. _____

   2. _____

   3. _____

   4. _____

4 Use the map for this question. Where is Mount Rushmore located in South Dakota?

    A in the west

    B in the south

    C in the east

    D in the north

5 Which face was carved second?

    A George Washington

    B Thomas Jefferson

    C Abraham Lincoln

    D Theodore Roosevelt

6 The faces are carved from _____.

    A sandstone

    B marble

    C granite

    D black stone

UNIT 4
Integration of Knowledge and Ideas

Identifying Connections

RI.3.8

When you read, how do you know you are reading facts? Where does the information come from? Sometimes, the author does not tell you the source of this information.

Can you tell facts and opinions apart? A **fact** is a something that you can be sure of. There is proof to support it. An **opinion** tells you how someone feels. Look for words like *best* or *worst*. These words can mean the author is not using facts. Words like *always* and *never* can mean this, too.

Do you use logic skills when you read? Can you see how some things cause other things to happen? Do you compare information? Do you look at the order in which things happen? Doing this can help you understand the things you read.

As you read, pay attention to what the author writes. Ask yourself questions as you read. Are you reading facts? Are you reading opinions? Do you see connections between sentences and paragraphs?

Guided Practice

Read the passage. Then answer the questions.

Cassie's Report on Landfills

by Cassie Davids

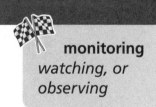

monitoring
watching, or observing

My report is about landfills. Landfills are areas that are designed to hold garbage and waste. They have to protect the air from things called pollutants. Pollutants damage the earth.

When you see a landfill, you might think that no one is monitoring it. But they do. People have to look out for the area. They have to make sure that no waste is getting into the ground water. They also have to make sure that no harmful gases are getting into the air. In fact, some newer landfills can take harmful gas and turn it into energy.

There is more to a landfill than just dumping garbage in a pile. First, the garbage is allowed to reach 3 feet tall. Then heavy machines flatten it. Finally, a layer of soil is put over the flat garbage. This soil is helps prevent odors and makes sure wind does not blow garbage around.

We need to have landfills. But there are too many of them! People need to recycle so that we do not waste any more land on landfills. Also, landfills are expensive. Something needs to be done!

Do you think that Cassie's report contains more fact or more opinion?

_____

_____

_____

 Think about what statements can be proven. Here is a sample answer:

Cassie's report contains many facts. Most of the report is fact. There are opinions at the end. For the most part, her report can be proven.

Which of these statements from the report is an opinion?

A We need to have landfills. But there are too many of them!

B Landfills are areas that are designed to hold garbage and waste.

C They have to make sure that no waste is getting into the ground water.

D The garbage is allowed to get to 3 feet tall. Then heavy machines flattened it.

You can prove what landfills are. You can prove that people check that nothing is getting into the water. You can also prove how tall the garbage is allowed to get and what they do with it when it gets tall. Choices B, C, and D are incorrect. Choice A cannot be proven. This is an opinion. The correct answer is choice A.

In this text, you can find an example of a sequence (things happening in a certain order). List an example of a sequence.

_____

_____

_____

Many times texts will have clue words for sequence. These are **first, second, third, then, finally,** and **after.** Here is a sample answer:

Paragraph 3 has an example of a sequence. It explains that first the garbage reaches 3 feet tall. Then it is flattened by trucks. Finally, it is covered with soil.

What is a difference between older landfills and some newer landfills?

_____

_____

_____

✓ Paragraph 2 explains some differences between landfills. Here is a sample answer:

Old landfills have to be watched. They might let gases get into the air. Many new landfills can turn harmful gas into energy.

If we start recycling, what will happen to our landfills?

_____

_____

✓ To answer this question we have to think about causes and effects. Here is a sample answer:

If we recycle our waste, we will have less trash. So this means that we will have less landfills.

Test Yourself

Dear Ms. Brown,

I am a third grader here at West Elementary School, and I love everything about it here. But I always have the same problem. I have so many books, papers, and things to keep track of that I lose my pens, pencils, and erasers. So I have a great idea.

I thought that maybe we could have a school store! We could open the store during lunch. Students could buy paper, pencils, pens, erasers, notebooks, and other things. And we could donate the money to the school or to a charity.

I have a friend who goes to another school. He has a school store that sells supplies. His school store is open every day. I think ours could just be open on some days, and that way, people do not spend too much money! It also makes it a fun, special thing for students to look forward to visiting!

supplies
items used by someone

A school store would teach us about counting money. It would teach us about responsibility. And it would help us understand how to best spend our money.

It would be easy to start a store. First, we would order some supplies. Second, we could set up a room during lunch to use as the store. Third, we train students to work in the store. Finally, we advertise to the school and hopefully get lots of sales.

Thank you for reading my letter. I hope you will think about letting us have a school store.

Thank you again,

Brittany Larson

1 What is Brittany trying to accomplish with her letter?

_____

_____

_____

_____

_____

2 Which of these is an opinion?

　A It would be easy to open a store.

　B His school store is open every day.

　C I am a third grader at West Elementary School.

　D He has a school store that sells supplies.

3 Which of these is an example of cause and effect?

　A I am a third grader here at West Elementary School, and I love everything about it here.

　B I have so many books, papers, and things to keep track of that I lose my pens, pencils, and erasers.

　C Students could buy paper, pencils, pens, erasers, notebooks, and other things.

　D It also makes it a fun, special thing for students to look forward to visiting!

UNIT 4 ✖✖✖✖✖✖✖✖✖✖✖✖✖✖✖✖✖✖✖✖✖✖✖✖✖✖✖✖✖✖✖✖✖✖✖✖
Integration of Knowledge and Ideas

4 Explain the sequence of events Brittany gives for starting the school store.

_____

_____

_____

_____

_____

5 How does Brittany compare and contrast her friend's school store to the one she wants to open?

_____

_____

_____

_____

_____

Comparing and Contrasting

RL.3.9, RI.3.9

Vocabulary
protests

There are many different kinds of literature. A narrative is a story. Most stories are made up. They are fiction. Some narratives can be true stories with facts. These are **nonfiction. Realistic fiction** is a made-up story that could happen in real life.

Traditional stories teach a lesson. These include fables, fairy tales, and folk tales. **Fables** are short stories that often have animals that act and talk like humans. They usually teach a lesson about how people behave. **Fairy tales** have elements of magic. They often include creatures like giants, wicked witches, and elves. **Folktales** are stories about ordinary people that teach a lesson about how people behave.

Have you ever noticed that some stories can talk about similar things in a very different way? Think about some common fables. Many fables have similar morals. "Honesty is the best policy" is one example. You can use different kinds of literature to prove the same point.

As you read, you should **compare** your texts. Think about how they are alike. What do the texts have in common? Also, **contrast** your texts. Think about how they are different. Maybe, it is the setting or characters. Noticing how stories are the same and how they are different will help you make connections. It will also help you better understand what you are reading.

The Story of the Wise Mother

a retelling of the Sudanese folktale

Once, long ago, there was a rich Sultan's son who lived with his mother. They lived in a large, fancy home. This mother was very wise, and her son was very lonely. The wise mother said to her son, "I know you long for a friend, my son, but be careful. You are rich, and many of the people you meet will become false friends. They will not be your friends because they love you. They will be your friends because they want your money. Do not let yourself get into this situation!"

The son kept these words in mind. Soon after that, he befriended a merchant's son. His mother advised him to bring the new friend to breakfast. She fixed it so that the breakfast arrived late, so the two men were very hungry. When breakfast arrived, it was nothing more than three boiled eggs. The friends each took one egg and ate it. Then the merchant's son picked up the third egg and gave it to the Sultan's son, who ate it. The Sultan's son thought this was very generous. But his mother did not agree. She said, "No, my son. He is trying to win you over so he can take advantage of you."

So the Sultan's son found a new friend, and again, his mother told him to bring the son to breakfast. The mother made the same plan. She made breakfast arrive late so that the two men were hungry. Again, breakfast was three eggs. This friend took the third egg for himself. The Sultan's son said, "Mother, is this better?" to which she responded, "No, this friend is selfish, and he will take your money."

Finally, the Sultan's son found a third friend, and this new friend was very poor. He was a hunter, and he hardly made any money. His house was a tiny shack, and his clothes were tattered. But the two men had a lot in common, they shared laughs, and they took part in the same activities. Finally, it came time for the two men to sit down to breakfast. When the mother brought three eggs to them, each friend ate one. Then the new friend took out a knife and split the third egg into two pieces. The Sultan's son was pleased. He looked to his mother for her approval. She nodded and said to him, "This is a true friend. Treat him well. It does not matter if he is rich or poor; he is a real and true friend. That is what matters." The two remained friends forever.

The Two Friends

a retelling of the Bura folktale

There once lived two mice. One mouse, Yizum, lived in the bushes in the woods. The other mouse, Nkinki, lived in the city. Yizum's food came from the forest. He ate simply, mostly seeds and grass. Nkinki's food came from rich houses. He snuck in and ate the leftovers from fancy family dinners.

When they met in the field one day, they decided that they wanted to see how each other lived. First, Nkinki visited Yizum's home. Yizum took his friend to eat dinner with him. Yizim was poor, so he presented his friend with a seeds and grasses that he found in the forest. But Nkinki did not seem pleased. "This food is so plain!" he exclaimed. "I do not like this simple food! You must come to my house!"

The next day, the two set out on another journey. This time, they traveled to a very large city. Once in the city, Nkinki said to his friend, "Look around you! Where would you like to go? We can go anywhere, and we can eat anywhere, and we can eat anything!" The two began to run toward a house. Suddenly, though, they heard something behind them. It was a cat! The cat chased them up and down the busy streets and empty alleys, and they ran until they were out of breath. When they had gotten away from the cat, Yizum said, "My friend, I know that you are rich and live in the city. I know you eat fine foods, but I could never do this. I could never be chased around all the time like this! I will choose my simple life."

Nkinki said, "You are a nice friend, but I feel the same about your place. Let us always agree to be friends and to visit each other. We enjoy different things, and we each love where we live. We can be friends in spite of our differences."

What is one common element in both of these passages?

A friendship

B greed

C mice

D forests

Both of these stories talk about friendship. Yet, they talk about friendship in different ways. One deals with animals. One deals with people. Both discuss what it means to be a friend. Choice A is the correct answer. Only one story talks about greed. Only one has a forest setting. Choices B, C, and D are incorrect.

What are three things that the two stories have in common?

_____

_____

_____

✓ **Think about what is the same about each story. Here is a sample answer:**

The stories are both about friends. They also both have rich and poor characters in them. Also, they show that people who are different can still be good friends.

What are three elements that are different between these stories?

_____

_____

_____

_____

✓ **This question asks you to contrast the two stories. How are they different? Here is a sample answer:**

One story is about mice. The other is about humans. In one story, the main character is trying to find a friend. In the second story, the mice are already friends. One text teaches a lesson about greed. The other teaches that friends can be different.

UNIT 4 ▓▓▓▓▓▓▓▓▓▓▓▓▓▓▓▓▓▓▓▓▓▓▓▓▓▓▓▓▓▓▓▓▓▓▓▓

Integration of Knowledge and Ideas

Passage 1

Man Walks on Moon!
July 20, 1969

Something amazing has happened on this day. Man has taken steps on the moon. We once thought this would be impossible. Today, Neil Armstrong announced this event with words that will be remembered forever: "The *Eagle* has landed," he said. What a thrilling moment it was when he took his first step onto the moon. He announced, "That's one small step for man, one giant leap for mankind."

That really is the truth. That one step that Neil took meant great things for the world. We will never again look at the moon and wonder "what if?" We will know that we have been there. We have seen it up close!

Armstrong described the moon's surface as a powdery sort of charcoal. Armstrong took soil samples and numerous pictures. Then, Buzz Aldrin joined him. The two collected data. They also tested the surface of the moon by walking and jumping on it. Finally, the two planted an American flag on the moon. The two also displayed a plaque to remember the event.

The two men spent 21 hours on the moon. They will return safely to Earth on July 24. This has paved the way for future space exploration.

Neil Armstrong Walks on Moon

Neil Armstrong was a member of the Apollo 11 crew. He and his crew landed on the moon on July 20, 1969. His crew included three people. Buzz Aldrin walked on the moon with Neil. The third man was Michael Collins. He was the pilot.

The two men had to wear space suits to walk on the moon. The suits had life support systems on them. The systems gave them air to breathe and controlled their body temperature.

The gravity on the moon is different than on Earth. For example, if the men jumped in the air on the moon, they could jump very high. On Earth, they could not jump as high.

The crew spent over two hours on the moon's surface. They collected samples and data to bring back to Earth to study.

The crew had planned ahead for their walk on the moon. They had a camera with them to provide live TV footage to the world. Everyone was able to see them on the moon. The men planted an American flag on the moon to remember this event.

What subject do these two passages have in common?

  A   men landing on the moon

  B   how to become an astronaut

  C   the clothing astronauts wear

  D   the history of the American flag

> Both texts are about the same topic. They both are about men landing and walking on the moon. They are written in different styles, but they are about the same thing. One is in the style of a newspaper article. One is in the style of a textbook entry.

What is a main difference between these passages?

_____

_____

_____

_____

> These articles are about the same topic. However, their styles are very different. Here is a sample answer:

The first passage is written like a newspaper article. It shows a bit of emotion with the facts. It is written with pride. The second one is just the facts. It does not present an opinion like the first passage.

How do the two passages work together to help you understand more about man's walk on the moon?

_____

_____

_____

_____

_____

_____

 Consider what is the same and what is different about the two passages. Here is a sample answer:

It is important to know the facts about events. But reading both passages gives the reader more. The first text gives an idea of the event's significance. The second text gives more information about the astronauts and their mission. After reading both texts, the reader has a better understanding of the event as a whole.

Martin Luther King Gives Stirring Speech

August 28, 1963

protests
organized disagreements about something

We have taken a step toward equal rights.

For too long, we have seen people treated badly. Much of this treatment is based only on skin color. Today, a speech was given that will go a long way toward changing this. At the Lincoln Memorial, Martin Luther King Jr. spoke of his wishes for this world. His words touched many of those who heard him speak.

King, a Baptist minister, has dedicated his life to equality among people. He dreams of a world where the color of one's skin does not matter. He dreams of a world in which all people are equal. So it was no surprise that his speech was titled "I Have a Dream."

Since the 1950s, King has been fighting for this cause. He and other equal rights supporters march and speak against things they do not agree with. They take part in protests that are not violent. They want their voices to be heard. King is respected by many people. He will make a difference.

Today, King was the last speaker at the March on Washington. Many famous people were at this march. They are all hoping for equal rights for all people. And they were all thankful for King's words.

Martin Luther King Jr.

Martin Luther King Jr. was born on January 15, 1929. He worked toward equal rights. King was very smart. He graduated from high school at the age of 15. He received his doctoral degree in 1955. He had two sons and two daughters with his wife.

In his life, King spoke more than 2,500 times. He traveled many miles. He moved many with his words. He believed in fair and equal rights for all people. This was not a popular idea at the time. He tried to change that.

In 1963, King spoke at the March on Washington. This was a large event. There were over 250,000 people there. The event was peaceful. This was important to King. He did not believe in using force. He believed in using words to show his beliefs.

At the march, King gave his most famous speech. This speech was called "I Have a Dream." In this speech, he talked about his dreams for all people. He talked about wanting them to have equal rights. He did not believe that skin color should matter.

King won a Nobel Peace Prize in 1964. He gave the money to his cause. His work touched many. But some people did not agree with it. In 1968, he was killed. But his work and his message will live forever.

1 Which of the following would describe both of the texts on pages 189 and 190?

   A They are both factual texts on the same subject.

   B They are both fictional words on the same subject.

   C They are about people who won Nobel Prizes.

   D They are about famous speakers who changed history.

2 Which of these *best* describes the difference between the two texts?

   A One is fiction and one is nonfiction.

   B One teaches a moral and one does not.

   C One is about Martin Luther King, and one is about his supporters.

   D One is about the "I Have a Dream" speech, and one is about Martin Luther King's life.

3 What is similar about the way the authors write about their topic?

_____

_____

_____

_____

_____

4 What is different about the way the authors write about their topic?

_____

_____

_____

_____

_____

5 Explain how reading both of these texts gives you a better understanding of the topic than reading just one.

_____

_____

_____

_____

_____

UNIT 4 ▨▨▨▨▨▨▨▨▨▨▨▨▨▨▨▨▨▨▨▨▨▨▨▨▨▨▨▨▨▨▨▨▨▨▨▨
Integration of Knowledge and Ideas

Integration of Knowledge and Ideas

UNIT

4

Vocabulary
benefit

Read two passages. Then answer the questions.

Passage 1

The Case of the Missing Lunch

This was going to be an extremely difficult case—one of the toughest I had ever had, but I knew I could handle it. No case was too tough for me.

My name is Jimmy Davies, and I am known to be something of a super sleuth among the students at Middletown Elementary School. When my friends or neighbors find something missing or have a mystery to solve, they come to me. I know just the right questions to ask, and I know just what clues to pick up on—and, I always solve my cases! When Sarah told me her lunch was missing, I knew I had to come to her aid.

"Jimmy!" Sarah said, "I do not know what to do. I just cannot find my lunch. I know I had it early this morning before I left for school, but when I got to school, I set my backpack down for just a minute. I went to put my lunch in my cubby, and it was gone!"

I nodded my head and scribbled some notes on my small notepad. "Anyone walk to school with you?" I asked. "Anyone ask you about your lunch?"

"No!" Sarah said. "What am I going to do? I am going to be so hungry at lunch—plus, there is a thief in our midst!"

I shook my head. "I will find him, Sarah… or her. I will definitely find out who did this!"

I started questioning my classmates, but they all shook their heads and denied having any involvement in this lunch theft. "No," they all said. "I would not take Sarah's lunch!" One of them even said, "No! I have leftover pizza for lunch, my favorite! Why would I take someone else's lunch?"

At the end of the day, I had not found the culprit. I shared my lunch with Sarah, because I felt bad about not coming through for her. I walked her home. When we went through her front door, I noticed something: there was a brown paper bag on the floor. It looks kind of like a bag you might take your lunch in. It was all torn up. I walked a bit further down the hall, and I noticed a plastic baggie with some punctures in it. The punctures looked a bit like teeth marks. Then I saw a chewed apple core sitting on the kitchen floor.

Just then, I saw Sarah's dog, Scooter. He noticed me looking him, and he looked guilty.

"Hey, Sarah," I said. "I believe I know who took your lunch!"

Passage 2

The New Dog

"Mom, please?"

"No."

"Please?"

"No!"

This is how my conversations with my family kept going, every time I asked for a dog. I was 9 years old, and all of my friends had dogs. I really, really wanted to have a puppy! I did not understand why we could not have one.

My parents told me that taking care of a puppy was a lot of work. They said that puppies needed to go outside all of the time and that puppies always had to be watched. They said that it was not all fun and games. I told them that I was 9 years old and that I was very capable of taking care of young animals!

UNIT 4 ✖✖✖✖✖✖✖✖✖✖✖✖✖✖✖✖✖✖✖✖✖✖✖✖✖✖
Integration of Knowledge and Ideas

Finally, my parents made a compromise with me. "Rachel," they said, "We know that you desperately want a puppy. We just need to make sure that you are really, really ready to care for it! You need to get some exposure to animals, first." So, my parents told me to volunteer at a local animal shelter. So that is just what I did!

On my first day, I was a little overwhelmed. There was a lot of clean-up to do! I also needed to take all of the dogs outside a lot. Some of them needed baths. They all needed feeding. My parents were right: this was a lot of work.

But then something amazing happened. I started to really get to know a new dog that had just come in. He was not a puppy; he was about 9 years old. His family had moved away, and they were not able to bring him with. The shelter was really nice, and everyone loved all of the dogs, but this dog really stuck with me. We became friends! I brushed his fur lovingly, and I always talked to him when I was at the shelter.

When I told my parents about him, they looked at each other and smiled. "Rachel," they said. "I know you wanted to pick out a puppy. But, it sounds like this dog has picked you!" I knew that they were right. There was something really special about bonding with this dog. And, even though I had thought I wanted a baby puppy, this dog was the right choice for me. My family adopted him, and he has turned out to be just perfect! (Though, just like a puppy, he does seem to really like the taste of shoes!)

1 "The Case of the Missing Lunch" and "The New Dog" both feature _____.

   A dogs

   B schools

   C mysteries

   D lunches

2 What is the same about the main characters in each story?

   A both want a dog as a pet

   B both want to find a missing dog

   C both try to solve their problems

   D both are helped by their parents

3 In passage 1, who stole Sarah's lunch? How do you know?

_____

_____

_____

_____

_____

4 How does the illustration in passage 1 help you understand the story's ending?

_____

_____

_____

_____

_____

Integration of Knowledge and Ideas

5 What sentence from passage 2 is *best* illustrated by the picture shown with passage 2?

   A My parents told me that taking care of a puppy was a lot of work.

   B But it sounds like this dog has picked you!

   C I brushed his fur lovingly, and I always talked to him when I was at the shelter.

   D Though, just like a puppy, he does seem to really like the taste of shoes!

6 List three differences between the two stories' main characters.

_____

_____

_____

_____

Passage 1

Shawn's Blog
Why We Should Walk More

It is about time that people started walking to work and school! Now, I will be honest. I love walking everywhere I go. My parents say that it is because I am young and I have so much energy. But I get tired from it! I get very tired by the end of the night. I know that I get that tired because I walk everywhere I go instead of getting a ride from my parents or taking the bus!

I have been telling people to walk everywhere for a long time. It is very important that we start walking more. First, walking is good exercise. And we need it! I live in Chicago, and the obesity rate here is 24%. That means that 24% of people need help getting their weight under control. Just imagine if they started walking to work or to school! It would help them a lot.

Also, think about the environment. Here in Chicago, it is no secret that pollution is a problem. The air just is not clean. And, why is the air not clean? One reason is pollution from cars. If fewer people drive cars, there will be less pollution. We will have fewer people driving cars if more people start walking.

Finally, walking is very relaxing. It gives you some quiet time to have to yourself. Or, if you are young like me, it gives you some good time with your mom or dad or other family members. Sometimes, my dad and I walk to get ice cream together. That is really fun, and it gives us a chance to talk, because it takes longer than driving.

So when you see people driving short distances, tell them to take a hike! Tell them the great reasons for walking. Even with all these great reasons, in Chicago, only 7% of people walk to work. We need to make that number grow!

Passage 2

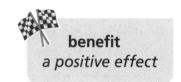

benefit
a positive effect

Walk for your Health

Research has proven that walking is good for your health. Experts have pointed out a lot of health benefits from walking. First, it helps you stay strong. It also lowers your blood pressure. Walking does not put a lot of strain on your knees. It also has been shown to help improve people's moods.

In the U.S., more than 64% of people are overweight or obese. A big part of this is that people do not get enough exercise. People give a lot of reasons for not getting enough exercise. One is the weather. People claim that the weather is not good enough for them to walk in. People in Illinois, for example, often say it is too cold or too hot for them to walk to work. Maybe that is why only 7% of Chicago people walk to work. Many of them drive. Some take the train.

People find a lot of reasons to not walk. But it is an easy exercise. You do not need to learn how to do it. You already know how to do it. Now people just have to take the next step and start walking.

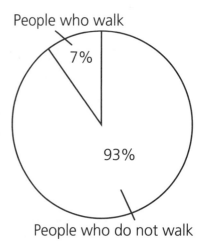

People who walk

7%

93%

People who do not walk

7 Which of these statements from passage 1 is an opinion?

   A It is about time people started walking to work!

   B I live in Chicago, and the obesity rate here is 24%.

   C If fewer people drive cars, there will be less pollution.

   D Even with all these great reasons, in Chicago, only 7% of people walk to work.

8 How does the pie chart help you understand passage 2?

_____

_____

_____

_____

9 How are the topics of the two passages similar?

_____

_____

_____

_____

10 What is different about the two passages?

_____

_____

_____

_____

PRACTICE TEST

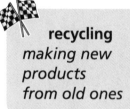

recycling
making new products from old ones

Read the passage. Then answer the questions.

Reduce, Reuse, and Recycle

You may have heard the terms *reduce, reuse,* and *recycle.* What do they mean and why do we need to understand them? The amount of waste we make has to go somewhere. If we want to help the environment, it is best if we reduce, reuse, and recycle.

What does it mean to reduce? Reduce means to "make smaller" or "use less." When we buy something at the store, we can make sure the packaging around it can be recycled. We can think about using the packaging for something else. It is also a good idea not to use single-serving containers. This is especially true for water. Do not buy bottles of water at the store. Buy a refillable sports bottle that you can fill. It is also helpful to buy in bulk, or in a large amount. Reducing the waste we produce will help the environment.

What does it mean to reuse? Do you ever use plastic forks and spoons? If you do, wash and use them again. The next time you have a lot of stuff to throw away, have a yard sale. Someone may want the things you do not need. When you go to the store, bring your own cloth bags instead of using the plastic bags at the store. If we reuse what we have, we will save a lot of room in landfills!

What does it mean to recycle? Recycling is making new products out of old ones. If a container can be recycled, do not just throw it in the trash. Put it in the recycle bin. Making new things from recycled items takes less energy than making them from new materials. You can recycle: magazines, soda cans, newspaper, glass, plastic, and many other things. Recycle your trash whenever you can!

We can all work together to reduce, reuse, and recycle!

1 What does it mean to <u>reduce</u>?

    A to make smaller or use less

    B to use again or more than once

    C to convert waste into reusable material

    D to return something to the store when you are done with it

2 Which of these is the topic sentence of paragraph 4?

    A Recycling is making new products out of old ones.

    B If a container can be recycled, do not just throw it in the trash.

    C Making new things from recycled items takes less energy than making them from new materials.

    D You can recycle: magazines, soda cans, newspaper, glass, plastic, and many other things.

3 If we buy something at the store and think about using the packaging for something else, we are thinking about the term _____.

    A reduce

    B reuse

    C recycle

    D reprint

4 What are the effects if we reduce, reuse, and recycle?

_____

_____

_____

_____

_____

5 Based on the article, which of these is *not* a benefit of reducing, reusing, and recycling?

   A takes less energy

   B less space is used up in landfills

   C using cloth bags means you can use them many times

   D takes a little more time to fill containers with water and food items from bulk container

6 From what you understand in the passage, what does the prefix *re-* mean?

   A again

   B harder

   C a little

   D no more

7 Write a summary of the passage. Include only the main ideas and most important details.

_____

_____

_____

_____

_____

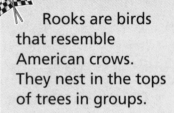

Rooks are birds that resemble American crows. They nest in the tops of trees in groups.

The Rooks

by Jane Euphemia Browne (1811–1898)

1 The rooks are building on the trees;
2 They build there every spring:
3 "Caw, caw" is all they say,
4 For none of them can sing.

5 They're up before the break of day,
6 And up till late at night;
7 For they must labor busily
8 As long as it is light.

9 And many a crooked stick they bring,
10 And many a slender twig,
11 And many a tuft of moss, until
12 Their nests are round and big.

13 "Caw, caw." Oh, what a noise
14 They make in rainy weather!
15 Good children always speak by turns,
16 But rooks all talk together.

8 Which words *best* describe the author's point of view?

   A Rooks are scary.

   B Rooks are lazy and messy.

   C Rooks are annoying.

   D Rooks are noisy and busy.

9 In lines 9–12, what picture was the author painting for the reader's mind?

   A rooks making noise

   B rooks coming back in spring

   C rooks building a nest

   D rooks cawing in the rain

Practice Test

10 In line 5, what does the phrase "before the break of day" mean?

   A just ahead of the sun rising

   B just after the sun starts rising

   C when the moon comes out

   D when the moon is full and bright

11 Read lines 15 and 16 from the poem.

Good children always speak by turns,
But rooks all talk together.

The author compares two things. Briefly explain the meaning of these lines based on the stanzas before it.

_____

_____

_____

_____

_____

Read the story. Then answer the questions.

The Ant and the Grasshopper

a retelling of Aesop's fable

It was a lovely summer day. Grasshopper was dancing and singing while he played his flute. Birds were chirping sweet songs as loud as they could. Butterflies were flying like kites blowing in the wind. Grasshopper was enjoying the day as if he did not have a care in the world.

As Grasshopper played, he spotted Ant carrying food into his house to store for winter. Grasshopper was surprised to see Ant working so hard.

"Come and sing and dance with me," Grasshopper said to Ant. "You do not have to work so hard. Let us have some fun together!"

"I have to store up food for the winter," Ant replied. "You should be storing food for winter, too."

"Oh, you do not have to worry about winter. It is very far away. I have plenty of time to store food," Grasshopper said.

Ant continued to carry food back to his home, shaking his head as he passed Grasshopper.

The cold and harsh winter came early. Snow fell and covered the ground. Ice formed over the pond. The bitter cold made it impossible to go outside.

While Ant was keeping warm, he heard a knock at his door. Grasshopper was standing outside, shivering.

"Would you please give me some food to eat?" Grasshopper asked Ant.

"I am afraid I cannot give you any food. You should have listened to me when I was storing food and done the same thing. It is best to prepare for the days ahead," Ant told Grasshopper.

12 Which of these is the *best* moral for this story?

    A Friends are not worth helping.

    B It all depends on your point of view.

    C It is best to prepare for the days ahead.

    D Don't ask anyone to solve your problems for you.

13 Why was Ant storing food for winter?

    A He was getting paid to do it.

    B He did not have anything else to do.

    C He wanted to have food to eat when it got cold.

    D He did not want to sing and dance with Grasshopper.

14 Which sentence from the story is an example of a simile?

    A Butterflies were flying like kites blowing in the wind.

    B Birds were chirping sweet songs as loud as they could.

    C Grasshopper was dancing and singing while he played his flute.

    D As Grasshopper played, he spotted Ant carrying food into his house to store for winter.

15 Do you agree with what Ant did at the end of the story? Explain your point of view.

_____

_____

_____

_____

_____

How to Keep Crows Out of Your Garden

Most gardeners think of crows as pests. Once crows move in, it is very hard to get them to leave. Farmers and gardeners use many ways to get rid of crows. Most ways work for only a little while. Keeping crows out of your garden is a full-time job.

Crows are very noisy. They are loud and annoying. Crows are also very smart birds. They are predators and scavengers. Crows are social birds. They work together. They will fight to protect their nests, eggs, and young.

Crows try to outsmart humans. They watch what is happening around them. They come around when people are not there to eat seeds, berries, fruit, and vegetables. They steal the eggs of nesting songbirds.

Crows store extra food. They bury it under grass or leaves and hide it in trees, rain gutters, and other handy places. They are attracted to ponds and birdbaths. They dunk their food in water before taking it to the nest. To keep crows out, a garden needs to be unattractive to crows.

An old-fashioned scarecrow is a great idea. Farmers used to use scarecrows hundreds of years ago, and they still work! Scarecrows should be human size and wear human

Did you know?
A large group of crows is called a "murder" of crows.

Key Words
social—live together in a group
outsmart—be smarter than
predator—animal that lives by stealing from other animals
scavenger—animal that eats food that is discarded by other animals or decaying flesh

Scarecrows in garden

clothing. Crows can tell if a face is human or not. Cover the scarecrow's face with a big, floppy hat. Crows are afraid of movement. Use a wig or yarn for hair that blows in the wind. Build a scarecrow that can be put in different positions. Move the scarecrow every day or so.

Crows do not like noise or shiny things. Hang wind chimes or old CDs in trees or on fence posts. In the wind, the flashes of light keep crows away. Punch holes in the outside edges of two tin foil pans. Sew them together with yarn or string. Before the final few stitches, place a few small rocks between the pans. Hang the pans across the garden. The shiny pans make noise and scare crows.

Try one thing at a time. Keep moving objects to new locations. When the crows return, try something else.

> For more interesting scarecrow ideas,
> visit http://www.makescarecrows.com/.

16 Which text feature on the page is *most* helpful to read before you start to read the text?

A hyperlink

B sidebar

C key words

D caption

17 What is the meaning of <u>old-fashioned</u> in paragraph 5?

A out of order

B broken down

C currently being used

D not used much anymore

18 Why does the author wait until the end of the passage to talk about scarecrows?

    A to first explain why crows need to be scared off

    B to first excite the reader into making a scarecrow

    C to help the reader understand the history of scarecrows

    D to help the reader know about other ways to scare off crows

19 Do you agree or disagree with the author's point of view on crows? Briefly explain your reasons.

_____

_____

_____

_____

_____

Read the two folktales. Then answer the questions.

Passage 1

The Smiling Rabbit

a retelling of the traditional Mexican folktale

There once lived a very poor old woman and a very poor old man. These two did not have much, but they did have a jaguar and a rabbit. One day they grew very, very hungry. They decided they were going to have to make rabbit stew because they did not have anything else. Well, the rabbit was not about to be made into stew! So he called the jaguar over. The jaguar came over smiling, and said "You are going to be stew, rabbit!"

"No," said the rabbit, "they are boiling water to make hot chocolate! Yum! If you rest quietly in my cage, you might get some chocolate. But if I stay in here, I will get the chocolate!"

The jaguar could not stand it, so he opened the rabbit's cage and let himself inside. The rabbit stepped out. "I will go get the owners," the rabbit said. The jaguar waited patiently, but the rabbit did not come back.

Finally, the jaguar left the cage. He went looking for the rabbit. He found the rabbit in a cave. He asked the rabbit what was going on. But, the rabbit said, "I am sorry, I do not know you. You must have me confused with someone else."

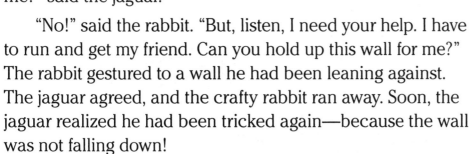

"So you are not the one who tricked me?" said the jaguar.

"No!" said the rabbit. "But, listen, I need your help. I have to run and get my friend. Can you hold up this wall for me?" The rabbit gestured to a wall he had been leaning against. The jaguar agreed, and the crafty rabbit ran away. Soon, the jaguar realized he had been tricked again—because the wall was not falling down!

The jaguar ran after the rabbit. "Come here!" he yelled, "come to me!" Finally, he found the rabbit, who was dangling from a vine. The jaguar went to pull on the vine to pull the rabbit down, but that plan really backfired! The rabbit flew up into the sky and escaped for good!

The rabbit had flown as high as the moon, and if you look closely, you can still see him there!

Turtle Tricks the Rabbit

retold from the traditional Native American folktale

Once, long ago, Turtle and Rabbit were walking through a field of long grass. "Hey, Turtle," said Rabbit. "I will race you through this grass."

"Okay," said Turtle, "though I fear I will lose."

"Of course you will surely lose!" Rabbit said gleefully. Rabbit was always saying these sorts of things, bragging about how fast he was. It made Turtle feel bad sometimes.

"But you are very short," Rabbit continued. "I will not be able to see you in the grass. You must wear a white feather on your head so that I can see you during the race."

"Okay," said Turtle.

But Turtle had a plan. That night, he visited his family. "Family," he said, "Rabbit has challenged me to a race. And I need your help to beat him!" He explained his trick to his family. The plan was this: each member of Turtle's family would wear a white feather on his head. They would stand at different locations through the race course. One would stand at the finish line. They would then pretend that turtle won the race.

The race time arrived. Turtle wore his white feather. When they started out on the race, Rabbit pulled ahead, as expected. Suddenly, Rabbit looked in front of him, and he saw Turtle! How could this be? So Rabbit ran even faster. Soon Rabbit saw Turtle ahead of him again! Little did he know that it was actually members of Turtle's family!

This pattern continued for the whole race. Finally, out of breath, Rabbit reached the finish line. But Turtle was already there. Rabbit realized he had been tricked! The trickster had been tricked!

20 What do the two story plots have in common?

   A both explain something in nature

   B both have characters who are clever

   C both include cooking some kind of dinner

   D both use a race as the main focus of the story

21 What is different about the themes in these stories?

   A One tells about eating a stew, and one tells about being in the stew.

   B One tells about winning a race, and one tells about losing a race.

   C One tells about climbing a wall, and one tells about flying over it.

   D One tells about getting tricked, and one tells about tricking someone else.

22 Read this sentence from passage 2.

   Soon Rabbit saw Turtle ahead of him again!

   What is another way of saying "ahead of"?

   A in front of

   B behind of

   C on the side of

   D head to head

23 Read this sentence from passage 1.

The jaguar waited patiently, but the rabbit did not come back.

What does it mean to wait <u>patiently</u>?

A to move around and suffer

B to stay in one place quietly

C to put up with something with anger

D to go through feelings of shame and guilt

24 Why did Turtle decide to trick Rabbit in passage 2?

_____

_____

_____

_____

_____

25 Explain what happens in the beginning, middle, and end of passage 2.

_____

_____

_____

_____

_____

Passage 1

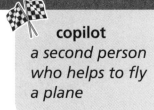

copilot
a second person who helps to fly a plane

My Report on Helicopters

Helicopters are amazing. They are meant to do very hard work. They can hover, or stay still, above an area. Airplanes cannot do that. Helicopters can pick up loads from the ground. They can even pick things up from the woods or move very heavy objects. They are powerful.

Helicopters use a lot of fuel. Some use up to 333 gallons of fuel per hour! They need to use all that fuel to lift up into the air. They have things called "rotors," which must spin in order for the helicopter to lift up. This is no ordinary vehicle!!

It is hard to tell how big helicopters are. To give you an idea, did you know that some of their blades are 30 feet long and three feet wide?

Helicopters are a lot more interesting than airplanes. There are almost 80,000 moving parts on some of them! It takes a pilot and a copilot to control it. They both have more than 150 control buttons to manage. It might be hard to be a helicopter pilot.

The Chinook helicopter is very powerful.

The History of Airplanes

What does the term "Kitty Hawk" mean to you? What about the Wright brothers? These are key words to know when you are learning about airplanes! In 1903, the Wright brothers flew the first plane. It was heavier than air. Yet, it still flew! Their work started years before. They did a lot of research before being able to fly the plane.

Today, there are many kinds of planes. There are stunt planes and sea planes, for example. Sea planes are interesting. They can land on water. Do you think that the Wright brothers ever imagined a sea plane?

Planes are used in many ways now. They are used for travel. They are also used for emergencies. The air force uses them.

Planes are different from helicopters. Helicopters can hover. Planes cannot do that because they are made differently.

Did you know that there are planes that can move at two times the speed of sound? And did you know that there are planes that fly at 13.5 miles above Earth? Planes that fly that high are collecting information about Earth. Planes have come a long way!

26 What does the photograph with passage 2 help you understand about the passage?

_____

_____

_____

_____

_____

27 Why do helicopters use so much fuel?

A because helicopters have to lift straight up into the air

B because helicopters have more than 150 control buttons

C because some helicopter blades can be up to 30 feet long

D because some helicopters need a pilot and a copilot to fly them

28 In passage 1, the author describes the helicopter as "no ordinary vehicle." What does the word vehicle mean in this sentence?

A a means for moving people and things

B a machine for flying up in the air only

C a movement that a machine would make

D a motor for a machine that would fly

29 Give three examples of facts used in passage 1.

_____

_____

_____

_____

_____

30 Compare and contrast these passages. What do these two
passages have in common? How do they differ?

_____

_____

_____

_____

_____

GLOSSARY

A

Alliteration   repeating the same consonant sounds

Allowance   sum of money given each week or month

Antonyms   words with an opposite meaning

B

Benefit   a positive outcome

Bough   tree branch

Bundles   bunches of things tied together

C

Cacao   seeds from which chocolate is made

Calculated   to determine

Century   a period of 100 years

Clinic   health center

Convince   to make someone feel sure

Copilot   a second person who helps to fly an airplane

D

Daylight Saving Time   time that is one hour later than standard time

Definitions   words that tell what another word means

Descriptions   words that tell you more about another word

Discrimination   unjust treatment because of race, age, or gender

E

Equal Rights   the same powers and privileges for everyone under the law

Excavating   digging

F — **Fact** — a statement or information that can be proven

Free verse — poem that does not rhyme or have a rhythm

G — **Government** — system that rules the country

H — **Haiku** — Japanese 17-syllable poem usually written in three lines

Hollow — empty

Homographs — words that are spelled the same but that have different meanings

Hosts — many

Hygiene — keeping clean of germs

Hyperbole — exaggerated statement for effect

Hyperlink — a link that uses the World Wide Web to find another source of information

I — **Idiom** — phrase that means something other than the literal meaning

J — **Justice** — fairness

K — **Key Words** — list of important words in a text

L — **Lawyer** — a person who practices or studies law; an attorney

Legacy — something that happened in the past that is passed on

Limerick — humorous rhyming five-line poem

Lyrics — the words to songs

 **Metaphor** — type of figurative language that compares two unlike things but does not use *like* or *as*

Monitoring — watching, or observing

Moral — concerned with the principles of right and wrong behavior

 **Nervous** — not calm, unsettled

 **Onomatopoeia** — words that sound like what they are describing

Opinion — something that someone believes or thinks

Outsmart — be smarter than

 **Personification** — giving human characteristics to a concept or inanimate object

Pinching — painfully cold

Plumed — covered in

Point of view — who is telling the story

   first-person — the main character is telling the story; uses first person pronouns *I* and *we*

   third-person limited omniscient — narrator is limited to knowledge of the thoughts and feelings of only one of the characters; uses third-person pronouns *he, she,* and *they*

   third-person omniscient — outside narrator is all-knowing and can reveal the thoughts and feelings of more than one of the characters; uses third-person pronouns *he, she,* and *they*

Predator — animal that lives by stealing from other animals

Prefix — part of a word added to beginning of another word that changes the meaning of the word

Protests — organized disagreements about something

Publisher — a person or company that prepares and issues books

R Recycling — making new products from old ones

Rhyme — repeated sounds at the ends of words

Rhythm — pattern of stressed and unstressed beats in a line of poetry

Robot — a machine that is able to carry out a series of actions

Ruddy — healthy, red color

Russet — reddish-brown color

S Scavenger — animal that eats food that is discarded by other animals or decaying flesh

Schedule — a timetable or plan for a certain time

Scorched — burned

Sidebar — short box printed on the side of text that has additional information

Simile — type of figurative language that compares two unlike things using *as* or *like*

Social — live together in a group

Sorrow — sadness

Standard Time — the official time of a country or region

Stanza — a group of lines within a poem, similar to a chapter within a book

Suffix — part of a word added to the end of another word that changes the meaning of the word

Supplies — items used by someone

Swallows — small, fast-flying birds

Synonyms — words that have a similar meaning

T Tend — take care of

Thrushes — family of songbirds, including robins

Time Zones — man-made areas around the world, each one hour apart

Translated — express words or text in another language

Vacuum   a device that collects dust and small things from floors

Wheatsack   bag of grain

Women's Suffrage   the battle for voting rights for women